The Forgotten North

The Forgotten North

A History of Canada's Provincial Norths

Ken Coates and William Morrison

James Lorimer & Company, Publishers
Toronto, 1992

Cover photos: Tessa Macintosh, R. Freeman

Canadian Cataloguing in Publication Data

Coates, Kenneth, 1956-
 The forgotten north

Includes index.
ISBN 1-55028-391-X (bound) ISBN 1-55028-390-1 (pbk.)

1. Canada, Northern - History. 2. Inuit - Canada.* 3. Indians of
North America - Canada, Northern. 4. Canada, Northern -
Economic conditions. 5. Canada, Northern - Social conditions.
I. Morrison, William R. (William Robert), 1942- . II. Title.

FC3956.C63 1992   971.9   C92-093757-8 F1090.5.C63 1992

James Lorimer & Company, Publishers
Egerton Ryerson Memorial Building
35 Britain Street
Toronto, Ontario
M5A 1R7

Printed and bound in Canada

Contents

Preface   vii

Introduction   1

1   The Sub-Arctic Fringe   11

2   The Incorporation of Northern Regions   33

3   The Colonizers' North   46

4   The Original Inhabitants   68

5   Completing the Colonization of
    the Provincial Norths   85

6   Divided Dreams: Perspectives on
    the Modern Provincial Norths   113

    Suggested Readings   133

    Index   137

Preface

Although there has not been a great deal written from a general perspective on Canada's Middle North — hence the impetus behind this book — we must give due credit to the scholars who have preceded us in this field, particularly Morris Zaslow, whose tireless dedication to northern history and determination to see that the region took its proper place in the study of Canadian history has been an inspiration to us since our student days. We have also been helped and inspired by the work of scholars from across the country who have swum against the historical currents to tell the story of a part of the country that most Canadian historians have overlooked, or never known; many of their names appear in this book's bibliography.

We have been helped in writing this book by a number of friends and institutions. The Centre for Northern Studies at Lakehead University provided vital financial assistance to get this project off the ground; the University of Victoria also offered research support which helped make completion of the book possible. We have benefitted immeasurably from the good advice willingly offered by Shelagh Grant of Trent University and Bill Waiser of the University of Saskatchewan, good friends as well as northern specialists, whose careful reading of the manuscript saved us from many errors and pointed us in useful new directions. They are not to be blamed for the book's mistakes, but are to be credited for much of what value it may possess. Many of our ideas were shaped as well through debate and discussion with Geoffrey Weller, formerly Vice-President Academic at Lakehead University, and now President of the University of Northern British Columbia. Few scholars have been as committed to the Canadian North, and particularly the Provincial Norths, as Geoff Weller; we have gained immensely from our association with him, which now, we are pleased to say, is moving off in a new and challenging direction.

We must, as always, thank our families for giving us the freedom and the inspiration to work on this project. Laura, Mark, and Bradley Coates, and Ruth and Claire Morrison have for some years now watched their fathers devote all too much time, perhaps, to wrestling with word processors; their patience and good humour in this respect deserves a greater reward than we can give them. Our wives, Cathy Coates and Linda Morrison, remain sources of strength and inspiration. We owe them a great debt for their willingness to support and encourage our research, particularly in the occasional dark days when the projects seem interminable and publication the light at the end of a very long tunnel.

When we started planning this book several years ago, we had no idea that the Provincial Norths would come to figure so prominently in our professional and personal lives. Bill Morrison had accepted a position at Lakehead University (whose motto, "A Northern Vision," demonstrated the institution's sense of itself as a northern university and its commitment to the region). Ken Coates, in contrast, taught at the University of Victoria, a first-rate institution, but based in Canada's least northern city. But all this has recently changed. In the early months of 1992, we both accepted positions at Canada's newest university, the University of Northern British Columbia, an institution dedicated to serving the needs of the citizens of northern part of that province. Once this happened, the ideas and opinions expressed in this book took on new meaning and significance. In fact, the research on this book went a long way towards convincing us of the necessity of a university in and for the North, as an important step in addressing many of the problems that we document in what follows.

And so, as if drawn by the writing of this book, we are heading off to the Prince George Campus of U.N.B.C., Ken Coates as Vice-President Academic and Bill Morrison as Dean of Research and Graduate Studies. If the readers sense any excitement in the pages of this book, it reflects our enthusiasm for the task ahead and our concern about the events which have created and influenced the development of the "Forgotten North." Finally, we are pleased that this book is the first to be published by faculty members at the University of Northern British Columbia. We hope that this will serve as a fitting start to the research and scholarly life of Canada's newest university.

Kenneth S. Coates,
William R. Morrison,
University of Northern British Columbia,
Prince George Campus,
May 1992.

Introduction

Canadians have always been fascinated by the North. But our interest has typically been limited to the "real" North of tundra wastelands, iceberg-filled waters, huddled musk-oxen, Inuit on Ski-Doos, Klondike gold miners, polar bears, artificial villages plunked on the ocean's edge, massive caribou herds, and Arctic explorers. These are the images that attract Canadians and inform our sense of nordicity. These form the subject matter for our artists, from Harris to Onley, our photographers, from Harrington to Hines, and our popular writers, from Berton to Mowat. It is this North, the Far North of the Yukon and Northwest Territories, that has seeped into our national subconscious and formed an integral part of our identity.

But this is not our only North. Canada has a vast sub-Arctic belt, running from the coast of British Columbia through the Canadian Shield and on to Labrador, that is surely northern by any objective standard, but which has been largely ignored by popularizers. Historians and other scholars have also tended to ignore this North; in only a few cases have systematic attempts been made to integrate it into a general understanding of the history of the provinces of which it is a part. In most survey histories, these Provincial Norths get a cursory glance at best. This book is an attempt to rectify this omission. It is about those other Norths, those great, ill-defined northern regions south of the sixtieth parallel.

With the exception of the Maritimes, all of Canada's provinces have sizeable northern territories, in some cases making up more than half of the provincial area — in Quebec's case, 80 percent. Long-ignored, politically weak, economically unstable, home to substantial aboriginal populations, these areas have played a significant, if relatively unknown, role in Canada's history. In the last three decades, southerners have once again discovered the untapped potential in these vast lands, and have rushed to develop the hydro-electric, mineral and timber resources in the sub-Arctic zones. But this is not the first time they have turned their attentions northward to regard not a sub-Arctic wasteland, but a land of opportunity. This wavering between neglect and enthusiasm, between southerners either anxious to develop northern resources or content to ignore the region, is a central theme in this study.

But this ambivalence is not the most important strain in the history of the Provincial Norths. Southern images of unin-habited wastelands, of rich forests, and mineral-bearing ground are in conflict with another reality, that of the aboriginal people. These lands are neither uninhabited nor abandoned — although some have been almost orphaned as a result of con-tact between indigenous peoples and Europeans. They are the homelands of the Native peoples of the Middle North — the Innu, Cree, Ojibwa and others — whose ancestors have lived for centuries in these allegedly inhospitable territories.

It is wrong to assume, as has so often been done in the past, that the issues of the Provincial Norths do not really affect Canada. Quite the contrary is true; it is possible to argue that many of the central conflicts and decisions facing Canada today originate in these regions, rather than from the settled south or the highly publicized "true" North. Because Canadians tend not to view the sub-Arctic band as a distinctive region within Confederation, they have typically ignored the tensions and debates that have emerged in the Provincial Norths.

Only a few minutes with recent newspapers and magazines provide numerous stories about conflict in this region, par-ticularly over issues involving Native people. While the In-dians and Inuit in the Yukon, Mackenzie River valley and Nunavut (eastern Arctic) have been celebrating very sig-nificant land claims settlements, Indians in the Middle North are still struggling for cultural survival without the benefit of such deals. The Innu of Labrador recently lost a court chal-lenge to stop low-level military flights over their homelands (but won by default when NATO decided that the decline of the cold war made the flights unnecessary); the Cree of Quebec are attempting to get the Province of Quebec to honour its obligations under the James Bay agreement and to prevent further degradation of their lands that may occur when the second phase of the Great Whale River project is constructed; the Teme-Augama Anishnabi of the Temagami region of northern Ontario are fighting desperately for control of lumbering and mineral development in their traditional lands; the Indians of northern Manitoba are still reeling from the devastation caused by massive hydro-electric projects; the Lubicon band in northern Alberta, battered and bruised after a difficult struggle, still seeks redress for its outstanding land claim; and in British Columbia, the Inganeka are attempting to rebuild a life torn asunder by the flooding caused by the W. A. C. Bennett dam, and the Gitskan Wet'suwet'en are immersed in a decade-long court challenge over their aboriginal land claim. The sad and significant fact is that this represents but a partial list of contemporary conflicts involving aboriginal peoples in the Provincial Norths.

Think now of the other side of the coin, of the developers' promises of resource riches and prosperity that would flow south from major northern projects, under way or proposed. The list is long, and the process is country-wide: proposed military training centres in Goose Bay, Labrador; further damming of the Churchill River; a massive extension of the James Bay power project; timber and mining activities (particularly the Hemlo field) in northern Ontario; continued hydro-electric development and more mining and forestry in northern Manitoba; controversial uranium mining projects in Saskatchewan; hotly-debated plans for massive pulp and paper developments and expansion of oil sands activities in Alberta; the false promise of north-east coal and new discoveries of gold in the extreme northwest of British Columbia. These are not small activities; they are the developments that generate much of the prosperity enjoyed in the southern parts of the provinces and are frequently hailed as the foundation for future growth in Canada.

Despite the number and variety of these contemporary issues, the Provincial Norths have not yet achieved a high political profile. Try to think of a nationally-known politician from any of these areas. There are some: C. D. Howe represented the region centered on what is now Thunder Bay, Ontario, as did both Robert Manion, briefly leader of the Conservative

Party, and Robert Andras, a member of the Trudeau government — but none of these was particularly identified as a
regional spokesman. Mackenzie King represented Prince Albert constituency at one time, but certainly seems to have had
little interest in northern Saskatchewan; even John Diefenbaker, who also represented the consituency, was not a spokesman for the region. An easier task: think of the name of a
provincial politician who came from, as opposed to merely
representing, a northern constituency. Some people may come
up with a name or two, particularly in their own province, but
few of these politicians will be of significant cabinet rank or
national prominence. The simple truth is that despite the national reputation earned by Elijah Harper of Manitoba for his
opposition to the Meech Lake agreement, the sparsely populated Provincial Norths are not well represented, either in their
own provinces or in the federal Parliament. Small populations
mean limited electoral power, which in turn ensures that in
Canada's system of brokerage politics, prime ministers and
premiers need not pay much attention to them. Because these
northern areas have a low provincial and national political
priority, the regions have been generally ignored.

Perhaps the best evidence of the weakness of the Provincial
Norths is the fact that there is virtually no sense of common
identity across the region. Each sub-region looks south for
social, political, economic and educational leadership. There
are few east-west connections, or bonds that might link the
various areas together — perhaps the national Native organizations and to a degree the environmental lobby. Unlike
the Far North, the Yukon and Northwest Territories, which has
a strong sense of identification with other circumpolar regions,
the Provincial Norths do not see themselves as a particular
entity within Canada.

Nor do most Canadians see them this way. Over twenty
years ago, Richard Rohmer attempted to popularize what he
called the "mid-Canada" corridor, seeking to draw attention
to the vast sub-Arctic band that dominates Canadian geography. He was unsuccessful, largely because these regions lack
the intrinsic interest of Arctic areas and, perhaps, because the
provinces have a vested interest in keeping their northlands
relatively powerless and unaware of their common history

and destiny. Canada is typically perceived as being divided into North and South, a simplistic description that ignores the sub-Arctic area that separates the populated zones (most within 100 miles of the Canada-U.S. border) from the land North of 60.

As a result of this pattern of systematic ignorance by governments, there has been almost no effort to deal with the Provincial Norths as special climatic or environmental zones. As one of the world's greatest northern nations (at least in size), Canada has a remarkable record of failure and inactivity in the areas of northern-based architecture, urban planning or environmental awareness. The northern provinces lack the population base, political clout or economic resources to study their own problems, let alone generate regional solutions. In this regard, as in many others, the Provincial Norths are significantly behind the supposedly more disadvantaged Yukon and Northwest Territories.

But this book is not simply an investigation of the contemporary challenges facing the northern regions of the Canadian provinces. The struggles and difficulties are not new; they can, in fact, be traced back to the emergence of the Canadian Dominion and to the northward extension of provincial boundaries. From the beginning in 1867, provincial politicians recognized the potential benefits from claiming and holding northern possessions, and they struggled long and hard to expand their hinterlands. Once politically incorporated into a provincial unit, the northern districts found themselves virtually powerless, lacking the political and economic authority to influence or control their destiny. Most of the non-Natives who came to live in the Provincial Norths cared little for the resulting pattern of underdevelopment and regional exploitation, as they were only sojourners in the sub-Arctic, seeking short-term jobs in the forests, mines and construction projects, and seldom staying long in the area. The aboriginal people were another matter, for, as wards of the Canadian state, they lacked even the most basic of political rights, and had, try as they might, little ability to influence the course of events.

As a consequence, the Provincial Norths have been developed with little system or view to the future. There are occasional bursts of enthusiasm about the regions. Individual governments offer their residents a short-lived vision of massive northern development, and some activity usually follows. Mines open, railway construction starts (and is sometimes completed), highways are built, forestry operations expanded and hydro-electric projects undertaken. But at the end of the day, little has changed, except that the Natives have been pushed off more of their land, many of the non-Natives have left, the land has been scarred, and little of lasting benefit has been left for the region.

What we are currently seeing in the Provincial Norths is, therefore, a continuation of a well-established process of systematic underdevelopment. The northern regions of the provinces have been rendered into internal colonies, their resources deemed to be available primarily for the benefit of non-Natives in the South, and with comparatively little thought given to the long-term prospects of northern society. The historical pattern, and current state, of much of the Provincial Norths offers yet another indictment of Canada's highly flawed, parsimonious, south-centred and urban-based approach to the Canadian North.

This, then, is a book about a part of Canada that most Canadians have chosen to ignore. It is about a region that lacks a regional identity, and in fact is made up of a series of units that have little contact with each other. It is about an area that holds much of Canada's resource wealth, and hence a good portion of its economic future, contains many of the country's poorest and most disadvantaged citizens (the majority of them Native), and has virtually no national voice or constituency. The pattern of perceiving the history and future of the individual Provincial Norths in isolation has prevented Canadians from identifying the broader significance of the Middle North, and from seeing the valuable lessons to be learned from our treatment of the land and people in this important region. It is essential to see the common links in the history of this vast and important land.

It is difficult to define the Provincial Norths, for there are many possible criteria for setting what are admittedly artificial boundaries. Numerous explanatory schemes have been advanced to identify the northern parts of Canada. W. L. Morton, for example, said that the line of commercially viable agriculture was the best demarcation between North and South. Geographer Louis-E. Hamelin constructed an elaborate scale of nordicity, which highlighted the difficulty of living in the northerly areas as the primary determinant. Other commentators have added other factors: the climate — equating extreme cold with northernness, a resource-based economy, political powerlessness and vulnerability, and a high percentage of aboriginal people in the population. Each of these factors has its attractions, and clearly no simple definition is going to suffice. Robert Bone, in *The Geography of the Canadian North*, lists the areas and populations of the northern regions of the provinces as follows:

Area of the Provincial Norths

Province	Area (000 km2)	Northern Area	% of Prov.	% of Canada
Nfld	406	300	74	3.0
Man	650	480	74	4.6
Sask	652	325	50	3.3
Alta	661	310	47	3.1
BC	948	375	40	3.8
Ont	1069	700	65	7.0
Qué	1541	1250	81	12.6
Total	5927	3740	61.6	37.4

Population of the Provincial Norths, 1986

Province and Census District	Pop. 1986	% Change since 1981	Major Urban Centre	Pop.	% Change since 1981
British Columbia	225,590	-0.1			
Bulkley-Nechako	37,470	-2.2	Smithers	4,713	3.0
Fraser-Fort George	89,337	-0.1	Prince George	67,621	0.1
Kitimat-Stikine	39,483	-6.9	Kitimat	11,196	-12.6
Peace R.-Liard	57,278	3.3	Fort St. John	13,555	-3.9
Stikine	2,022	3.5	Stikine	1,750	1.6
Alberta	97,631	11.4			
Division 16	48,779	11.9	Ft. McMurray	34,949	12.7
Division 17	48,852	10.9	Slave Lake	5,429	20.5

Saskatchewan					
Division 18	25,340	0.1	La Ronge	2,696	4.5
Manitoba	73,996	0.1			
Division 19	9,125	-25.7	Berens River	803	17.9
Division 21	24,068	-2.6	The Pas	6,283	-1.7
Division 22	30,544	14.5	Thompson	14,701	2.9
Division 23	10,259	2.5	Leaf Rapids	1,956	-17.2
Ontario	434,060	-2.2			
Algoma	131,841	-1.3	Sault Ste Marie	80,905	-22.0
Cochrane	93,712	-3.3	Timmins	46,657	1.2
Kenora	52,834	-11.1	Kenora	9,621	-2.0
Thunder Bay	155,673	1.1	Thunder Bay	112,272	-0.2
Quebec	473,326	-3.0			
Abitibi	94,410	0.1	Val-d'Or	22,252	3.8
Chicoutimi	174,625	0.1	Chicoutimi	61,083	1.5
Lac-St-Jean-Ouest	62,977	0.0	Roberval	11,448	0.5
Saguenay	104,131	-10.1	Baie-Comeau	26,244	-2.3
Terr.-N.-Qué	37,183	-9.6	Chibougamau	9,922	-7.5
Nfld.	54,695	-4.1			
Division 9	25,954	-4.1	St. Anthony	3,182	2.4
Division 10	28,741	-8.2	Labrador City	8,664	-24.9

This table shows that many regions of the Provincial Norths suffered population declines in the first half of the 1980s. In most cases the decline was due to conditions in the resource sector during the serious recession of those years.

There are strong historical forces that have to be taken into account in each province. The relationship between the southern areas and the northern hinterland is, for example, a crucial determinant of the pattern of social and economic development. In some provinces, such as Ontario, Saskatchewan, and Manitoba, departments of northern affairs have been created, and the area of their responsibility obviously indicates that province's political definition of the northern zone.

Using these standard means of identifying northern areas, however, both creates and ignores some important anomalies. The land around Dawson Creek and Fort St. John, British Columbia, for example, is excellent for commercial agriculture. Is this area, which is hundreds of miles from the centres of provincial power, subject to very cold winters and tied into the economic insecurities of oil and gas development, therefore not to be considered northern? Similarly, the city of Thunder Bay would not make it very high on Hamelin's list of nordicity, but despite its industrialization and high level of services it clearly sees itself as a northern centre, particularly as the hub of northwestern Ontario. Should it be left off?

It seems, in fact, that the best means to determine northerness is to look to the specific cases, and to recognize that nordicity can, and does, change over time and across regions — not due to global warming, but because of shifts in economic and political circumstances. Or to put it another way, northerness is to a considerable degree in the eye of the beholder. The Provincial Norths do share some common characteristics: their land is generally cold and (with important exceptions) does not support commercial agriculture; they have little political power at either the provincial or federal level; their economy is heavily resource-based and therefore subject to extreme fluctuations; there are very few people scattered across vast lands; the non-Natives are typically restricted to a small number of regional centres; there is a large aboriginal population that is generally relegated to a few specific sectors in the resource economy; and the non-Native population is notable for its mobility.

The Provincial Norths have also had strikingly similar histories. Whether in Labrador, northern Ontario, or in northern British Columbia, the control exerted by outsiders, the impoverishment of the indigenous population, the emphasis on rapid, profit-oriented development, and the inability of local residents to control their destiny are readily evident.

The purpose of this book is to draw these disparate strands together, and to identify the distinctive pattern of development and change in the Canadian Provincial Norths. An important theme will be the process by which these long-ignored peripheral regions in Canada have been incorporated into the broader Canadian economy and society in such a way that the primary benefits from the development of regional resources have flowed out of the region and into southern hands. The point, put simply, is that the northern regions have become internal colonies of the southern population, with massive transfers of wealth out of the region and with comparatively little attention being paid to the inhabitants, indigenous or newcomers, of the northlands. Time and time again, from the early mining activities to contemporary hydro-electric mega-projects, the so-called "provincial interest" has over-ridden regional concerns and priorities, establishing a pattern of underdevelopment and impoverishment that remains, today, as the principal characteristic of Canada's Provincial Norths.

Chapter One

The Sub-Arctic Fringe

The region we have labelled the Provincial Norths is majestic, stunning, relatively unpopulated and unpolluted and, to most Canadians, largely unknown. It comprises well over a third of Canada's land-mass and has long played a pivotal role in the evolution of human habitation in the northern half of North America. But this region that stretches from Labrador to northern British Columbia defies easy description, because it is not a single geographical, physical or historical zone.

There are some physical characteristics that are common to most of the region. It is ruled, to a large extent, by its geology. Thousands of millions of years ago, in a geological period called the Precambrian age, before there were any trees or plants of any kind on earth, the great Canadian Shield was formed. It is ancient rock; in fact, as of this writing the oldest rock samples ever found on earth — some 3.9 billion years old — come from the Shield. It is Canada's principal geological feature, covering almost 1.8 million square miles. It is the kernel not only of Canada, but of all North America, and covers almost all of the Provincial Norths. Only the greater part of northern Alberta, which is a geological extension of the Great Plains, and British Columbia, which was formed by tectonic pressures from the Pacific, lie outside the Shield.

Southern assumptions about the Provincial Norths reflect the belief that the region has always been cold, and that the current climatic norms represent permanent conditions. In terms of geological time, this is simply not true. The physical mass that now constitutes Northern Canada has not always been as near to the North Pole as it is now, and has thus not always been a region of extreme cold and snow. In the Carboniferous period, what is now northern Canada was close enough to the equator for tropical forests to grow and then decay into the petroleum and gas deposits of northern Alberta, the Mackenzie Valley and the Beaufort Sea. The mummified trees recently found in the extreme North, on Ellesmere Island, bear silent witness to the broad and startling sweep of climatic change over the eons.

Continual shift of continental plates over millions of years moved the continents to their present positions and created the physical distribution of land mass that we often mistakenly assume has been permanent. In the comparatively recent geological past, a series of massive ice sheets pushed outward from glacial caps, covering almost all of Canada. The ice lay deep over the land — hundreds of metres of ice continuing for hundreds and hundreds of kilometres — scouring the soil and rock that lay underneath. The detritus of glaciation was scraped off northern Canada and deposited as topsoil in what is now the northern United States. The eskers and drumlins which dot the landscape of southern Ontario, as well as the innumerable rocks which pop to the surface of prairie farms every spring, are legacies of the glacial era. Another legacy is the general physiography of the Provincial Norths.

The last period of glaciation, the Wisconsin, occurred some 18,000 years ago, creating the basic structure of the Provincial Norths. The advance and retreat of the glaciers recast the area. As the glaciers pushed south, colliding with the hard rocks of the Canadian Shield, they ground down the hills and mountains, creating the relatively flat landscape that now dominates the region. The ice sheet also scoured out the myriad pot-hole lakes that freckle the landscape.

A slow warming of the world's climate caused the retreat of the Wisconsin glacial sheet, providing a more favourable environment for plant life and, consequently, animal and human occupation. But the glaciers left little behind — a thin veneer of soil over the rocky face of the Canadian Shield — and new life moved slowly back into the ecological vacuum. For many years, with the glacial sheet retreating northward, the land lay fallow and empty, devoid of the plant and animal life necessary for human habitation. Over time, in remarkable testament to the adaptability and tenacity of life on earth, plants, birds, animals and other life forms moved slowly into the region. To the south, on the Great Plains and around the

Great Lakes, where rich soils combined with warmer temperatures, the enrichment of the vacated lands occurred faster and
was more diverse. In the northern zones, where the weather
remained cool, and where the glaciers had left plants, animals,
birds, fish and other organisms little to work with, a more
simple ecology emerged.

The southern limit of the Provincial Norths is imprecise, and
scholars have defined it in different ways. A reasonable definition would be the vague line between southern lands, where
commercial agriculture is possible, and northern lands, where
no such prospects for extensive cultivation exist. The emphasis
on "commercial" agriculture is deliberate, as there are small
pockets of arable land in the North, usually in river valleys.
But a small home plot of potatoes near Athabasca or Norway
House, or a hayfield near Fort Nelson is not enough to suggest
that these regions are other than northern. This broad gener-
alization naturally has some important exceptions. The finger
of rich land in the Peace River country of northern Alberta and
British Columbia and the promising clay belt in northern Ontario were blessed with rich soils and hence, in the years after
European settlement, attracted their share of farmers. With
these exceptions — and a certain amount of fuzziness along
the boundary between the agricultural zones of the St.
Lawrence River valley and Nouveau Québec — the general
boundary holds: the northern provinces are defined (though
not very precisely) in their southern extremities by the line of
commercial agriculture.

The northern boundary of the Provincial Norths is easier to
define in the East, though geographically artificial in western
Canada. For Newfoundland, Quebec and Ontario, the provinces extend northward to large bodies of water. The Atlantic
Ocean, Hudson Strait and Hudson Bay provide logical, natural
lines of demarcation between the northern provinces — the
Mid-North — and Canada's other North, the Yukon and
Northwest Territories. From Manitoba westward, the Provincial Norths end with a line drawn for political rather than
geographical or geological reasons. There is nothing important
to differentiate the extreme north of Manitoba from contiguous
regions of Keewatin; northern Alberta is very much a part of
the upper Mackenzie Valley. Northern British Columbia, sep-

arated physically from the east by the northward thrust of the
Rocky Mountains, is geologically bound to the Yukon Territory to the north.

There is, consequently, no easy physical rationale for drawing the northern boundary of the Mid-North — unless, of
course, one adopts the definition used by Richard Rohmer in
his study of the Middle North, in which he emphasizes geological features over political and other factors. In Rohmer's
conception, the Middle North is defined as the vast Canadian
Shield and sub-Arctic region of the country, and thus comprises part of the territories as well as the Provincial Norths.
But for reasons that will become more obvious as this book
proceeds, there are important non-geological reasons for
differentiating the Provincial Norths from the Territorial
North.

Latitude, which many Canadians use as a yardstick for climate and harsh living conditions, is of little value in attempting to define the Provincial Norths. Consider a few of the more
obvious anomalies, which perhaps point to the need for geographical literacy in attempting to understand Canada. Moosonee, Ontario, which is certainly part of the Provincial
Norths, lies further south than do Edmonton, Alberta and
Prince Albert, Saskatchewan, which are not. Sioux Lookout,
Ontario — in the Provincial Norths — is on the same parallel
as the agricultural centre of Regina, Saskatchewan. Timmins,
a mining centre in northern Ontario, is on the same latitude as
Victoria, British Columbia, a city whose boosters' proudest
boast is that their community is the least northern in Canada.

Although the definition of the Provincial Norths highlights
the importance of the Canadian Shield and the absence of
commercial agricultural prospects, these factors alone do not
really clarify an understanding of this little-known region.
Consider the tremendous diversity of land contained within
it. The northernmost limit of the Provincial Norths is at the tip
of the Ungava Peninsula, substantially north of the sixtieth
parallel and an area that is Arctic by any definition. The southern limit of the region, several hundred miles to the west and
more than a thousand miles to the south, is in northern Ontario, around the forty-fifth parallel. And the diversity extends
far beyond the variation from north to south. The stunning

majesty of Atlin, British Columbia, a brilliant, mountain-sur-
rounded jewel in the northwest corner of the province, bears
little resemblance to the mosquito-plagued lakes and vast pine
carpet of northern Ontario. In the East, along the coast of
Labrador, deep fiords, buffeted by frigid North Atlantic
winds, present an imposing visage, in contrast to the gently
rolling hills of the Peace River country of northern Alberta and
northern British Columbia. Stereotypic images of the region,
therefore, miss its geological range and variety.

Much of the life and activity in the Provincial Norths centres
on the region's many dominant waterways. Its powerful,
dangerous rivers have historically exerted a tremendous influence on the region (and, as debates over hydro-electric
development show, continue to do so today). The rivers — the
Churchill in Labrador, Great Whale and Eastmain in Nouveau
Québec, the Albany and Atiwapiskat in northern Ontario, the
Hayes, Nelson and Churchill in Manitoba, the North Saskatchewan in Saskatchewan, the Peace in northern Alberta and
northern British Columbia, and the Stikine and Skeena in
northern British Columbia — are massive conduits, draining
vast territories. There are few large lakes in the area — some
of the largest now are artificial ones created by hydro-electric
dams — but an uncounted number of small lakes, dotting the
rocky landscape that makes up so much of the Canadian
Shield.

It is easy to dwell on the variations within the Provincial
Norths and to ignore the commonalities that unite the region.
Much of it is characterized by expanses of flat bush country or
low mountains and hills — a drive to Chisasibi, Quebec, to
Thompson, Manitoba, to Fort Chipewyan, Alberta, or to Fort
Nelson, British Columbia will confirm this impression —
covered with a seemingly endless carpet of sub-Arctic ever-
greens. In the southern extremities of the region, these trees
have commercial potential, providing the engine for economic
development in much of the area. In colder climates, as in
northern Quebec near the tree line, the commercial prospects
of the timber diminish.

The vast landscape of the Provincial Norths invites fantasies
of unlimited richness and opportunity that seriously overstate
the reality of its economic potential. The sub-Arctic climate of

much of the region imposes severe limits on the possibilities for plant and animal life. The trees that dominate the region, for example, grow slowly; it is the existence of tens of thousands of acres of harvestable timber, rather than the richness of the resource itself, that makes commercial timber operations possible. The sub-Arctic region does not have the biological diversity of more southern zones. There are fish in the rivers and lakes, but not in the numbers and variety of more benign ecological areas. Similarly, the forests are home to many animals, birds and plants, but of few species, compared to warmer regions. A few major species of game animals dominate — moose and deer across much of the region, caribou herds in a few places (particularly in Nouveau Québec), and there are a significant number of fur-bearing animals, including the fabled beaver, the unglamorous but more abundant muskrat, and such luxury fur-bearers as the marten, lynx, bear, and wolf. There are many birds, notably the massive flocks of migratory birds — particularly geese and ducks. But the sub-Arctic regions host comparatively limited indigenous animal and bird populations year-round, and they are vulnerable to changes to their ecological niches.

The sub-Arctic climate dominates the region but, again, generalizations collide with regional realities. Not all of the areas are equally cold — Fort St. John has a warmer climate than Fort Churchill, and Thunder Bay and Moose Factory have much different climates — and the grip of winter lingers much longer in some areas than others. Remember that the definition of the Provincial Norths includes such diverse areas as the tip of the Ungava Peninsula and the Peace River country. Winters are cold, in some places extremely so, with temperatures falling to -40 °C or colder for several weeks each winter. Growing seasons are much shorter than in the south, although some partial compensation is found in the length and warmth of the summer days.

The Provincial Norths contain vast, not yet fully defined mineral wealth in both the Canadian Shield and non-Shield areas. Over the last century, prospectors and miners have tapped into these deposits, uncovering the rich gold pockets across the region, iron ore in Nouveau Québec, coal in northern British Columbia, nickel and gold in northern Ontario and northern Manitoba, uranium in northern Saskatchewan, and other minerals throughout. These resources, with the exception of copper, were not utilized by the indigenous inhabitants, and lay buried still and rich in the land, waiting for newcomers of materialistic and industrial bent to come in search of the wealth.

Bearing in mind the diversity within the area, the Provincial Norths can be defined by certain physical characteristics: they are certainly colder than the rest of the country (except for the Arctic regions), are dominated by a series of major rivers, and incorporate a vast sweep of non-agricultural, heavily treed land. The region contains much biological wealth in its rivers, lakes and forests, although the ecology is limited in diversity and is considerably vulnerable to change. Age-old geological forces left mineral deposits buried deep in the rocks — perhaps not as much wealth as later promoters would promise, but in abundance nonetheless. It is a land of surprising complexity and diversity, a region that is impressive by its very size, and the stature of its rivers, mountains and winter climate. The land and sub-Arctic climate would, of course, impose limits on human occupation of the land and would determine much of the shape and nature of settlement in the area.

But the Provincial Norths are not defined by geological and biological characteristics alone. While contemporary rhetoric likes to paint the Provincial Norths as "new" land, a region of the present and future, the region has in fact been the homeland for a diversity of indigenous societies for several thousand years. These people lived on and with the land, and did not attempt to change or exploit it, in sharp contrast to the newcomers who would arrive later. Theirs was a unique, much misunderstood occupation of the sub-Arctic regions, one worth considering in some detail.

Our understanding of the indigenous societies of the sub-Arctic, aided tremendously by the work of several generations of ethnographers and anthropologists, and by the willingness of Native elders to speak about their history and culture, remains far from complete. We know very little about the first centuries of occupation, but the level of understanding improves steadily, though imperfectly, as we move toward the present. There is a tendency to see the years before European contact as an undifferentiated whole, with the indigenous peoples changing little over time. This assumption is both incorrect and misleading, for it suggests that the original inhabitants were unaccustomed, and by implication unwilling, to change.

The peoples who first inhabited the sub-Arctic arrived not long after the last glaciers retreated, about 8000 B.C., although the entire region was not occupied at the same time. Some areas — the Ungava Peninsula and the coast of Labrador, for example — did not see human settlers until centuries later. The migration across North America, which began as the great ice sheet retreated northward, initially headed southward toward more salubrious climates. Later, as lands to the south were more fully occupied, people moved northward. But they did not wait to do so, as one might assume, for generations after the ice age. As recent discoveries in northern Ontario have shown, indigenous peoples pushed up against the retreating southern fringe of the retreating ice. The most northerly path of migration, that of the Dorset and Thule peoples, ancestors of the contemporary Inuit, came much later (around 4000 B.C.) and, from available evidence, moved west to east across the Arctic. Warmer weather at the time permitted people to move into the high Arctic Islands; when colder temperatures settled in, the people moved south, including into what is now northern Quebec and Labrador.

Little is known about these early peoples; they are known in academic circles primarily by their tool technology and are defined by the small number of archaeological sites discovered to date. Given what we do know about the geography, climate and resources of the Middle North, it is likely that their basic way of life differed little from that of their descendants who occupied the region at the time of contact with Europeans. There were changes, such as the introduction of the bow and arrow, that brought significant shifts in harvesting technology and, consequently, in social and personal relations. The societies were not static, but the shifts and reorganizations that occurred were slight, for in the period from 2500 B.C. to A.D. 1500 there were few major ecological changes. As anthropologist Alice Kehoe has pointed out, of all of the "Late Archaic" populations, that of the Canadian Shield persisted most strongly "because it adapted well to a relatively harsh environment that has allowed few alternatives to the humans who live on it" — at least until Europeans, with their sense of supremacy over the land, arrived. Once the indigenous peoples had developed a means of sustaining life by hunting caribou and other large mammals, and had created the canoe and other material necessities of life, they had established a level of adaptation to their environment that could not readily be improved upon — at least not without major technological innovation or sweeping and serious repercussions for the ecosystem. Thus, according to Kehoe, "the contemporary Cree and other Algonkian-speaking peoples of the Shield forests exhibit a Late Archaic cultural pattern."

While these observations suggest a certain stasis in aboriginal culture in the North, they mask, again, the diversity of indigenous life. Because the Provincial Norths' many ecosystems varied widely, indigenous societies developed with pronounced differences. At the most extreme — and not suggesting that the cultures can be ranked according to any artificial scale of sophistication or "civilization" — the cultures ranged from the hierarchical and semi-sedentary Nisga'a of northwestern British Columbia to the mobile Cree of northern Manitoba and the much smaller Inuit cultures of northern Quebec and Labrador. The First Nations of the Middle North can be divided into five basic groups (and dozens of smaller nations): the Algonkians (Montagnais, Innu, Naskapis, Cree and Ojibwa) who lived principally in northern Ontario and Quebec; the Dene or Athapaskan peoples (including the Chipewyan Beaver, Tahltan and Carrier) of the northern Prairies and British Columbia; the Northwest Coast cultures of northwest British Columbia (including the Inland Tlingit and Tsimshian); and, in northern Quebec and Labrador, the Inuit peoples.

Many hundreds of years after the indigenous people arrived, Europeans would describe these cultures in unflattering terms. These images and attitudes can be attributed to their inability and unwillingness to recognize the nature of aboriginal societies; the inaccuracy of many, if not most, of the early descriptions means that characterizations of indigenous cultures must be advanced cautiously. It is worth considering, as a starting point, the remarkable longevity of these societies. Even when the Europeans arrived, they were not, by any means, "new" peoples, for they could trace their ancestry in a particular region back for millennia. Even the Inuit — the relative latecomers in the pantheon of indigenous cultures in North America — began to arrive some six thousand years ago, four thousand years before Jesus Christ walked through Jerusalem, and several centuries before the Egyptian pharaohs started work on the first pyramids. European societies thus appear as infants when compared to the longevity and persistence of the indigenous peoples of northern North America.

Contrary to the widely held perception of the first peoples of northern Canada, the indigenous societies were not simply impoverished versions of their southern counterparts such as the Iroquois, Nuu Chah Nulth and Micmac. It is simply not true that because the indigenous peoples of the Provincial Norths lived, in the years before contact, in environments that were more challenging than those in more temperate climates, that they were therefore entrapped in a life of perpetual hardship and continual struggle for survival. The anthropologist Marshall Sahlins argued some years ago, in a provocative article entitled "The Original Affluent Society," that the lives of the hunter-gatherers of the world were not, in the famous phrase of Thomas Hobbes, "nasty, brutish, and short." Material prosperity is a philosophical rather than an absolute state, he argued, and wanting few possessions is just as good a cure for materialism as gaining many; better, in fact, since there is no limit to human greed. More important, the indigenous peoples in the Middle North were hunter-gatherers, who relied on seasonal movement, dictated by the availability of resources, for survival. Material possessions, consequently, were a hindrance to them. These people, like the Aborigines in Australia, provided for their basic needs with considerably less effort six hundred years ago than did most of their European contemporaries, and were generally better fed.

While the indigenous peoples did not covet material abundance, they did seek some things to which they attached tremendous value — leisure time and the ability to travel. If they could provide for their food needs with relative ease — and

their movements and knowledge of resources generally ensured that this was possible — the aboriginal peoples could
devote their time to preferred pursuits, including story-telling
and cultural activities. Sahlins, in defining affluence, wrote
that it means the ability to achieve a culture's goals, and not,
except in western, capitalist societies, the ability to control
material or financial wealth. Judged by this standard — the
ability to satisfy the cultural objectives — the indigenous
peoples of the Provincial Norths were "affluent," although few
Europeans recognized them as such.

The Provincial Norths were not, as many might imagine,
desolate regions over which scanty populations moved, con-
stantly on the brink of starvation, scrounging for scraps of food
wherever they could. Instead, the indigenous peoples lived in
self-contained worlds, where they enjoyed full rather than
desperate lives, well-fed on the species of fish, game animals
— caribou, moose, deer, seal — birds and plants that lived in
their part of the continent. The people were not concentrated
in one area, in the way that the Pacific Northwest coast hosted
a large population, or the Aztecs took advantage of their rich
lands and developed massive cities, but they were not as few
in number as scholars long assumed; a recent estimate of
population of the Provincial Norths plus the Yukon and Mackenzie Valley at the time of contact is 40,000. The hunter-
gatherers lived within the means of their surroundings,
limiting the size of their communities and relying on movement within their territories to ensure a steady supply of food.
Indigenous groups also developed extensive trading connections with contiguous and even distant peoples, exchanging
surplus commodities — fish, pelts, certain varieties of meat,
metal, flint or other goods — for materials not available within
their own lands. The cultures were, consequently, able to provide for their limited material and food needs and did so
without spending their entire lives in an endless pursuit of the
food necessary for survival.

It would of course be equally incorrect to err in the opposite
direction, and to suggest that the indigenous peoples lived in
a "Golden Age," in which there was no suffering, hardship or
shortage of food. There were occasional problems — no society
at any place or any time has been granted absolute security

and fully equitable distribution of resources — and suffering was not unknown. Periods of unusual cold, floods, forest fires, or unexpected depletion of animal resources could cause immediate, and sometimes fatal, difficulties. But it is important to remember that such things happened in other societies, including Europe in the age of North American discovery. Conflict with other societies could also disrupt food gathering activities and cause starvation. These were not idyllic societies — which is? — but they were far less deprived and much less likely to experience hardship than popular and scholarly wisdom long assumed.

The indigenous societies and cultures of the Provincial Norths were complex and diverse. They varied widely in terms of language, fundamental beliefs, social organization, and other societal attributes. The peoples ranged in social complexity from the family-centred Inuit peoples to the more hierarchical Tsimshian societies. The Algonkian and Dene peoples lived in relatively small band societies, although most lived in extended family units for much of the year, coming together as season and culture dictated and as harvestable resources allowed. The people believed that all aspects of their world were filled with spirits, and did not see themselves as being separate from, or superior to, the animal, plant and physical environment that surrounded them. Each group had spiritual leaders — healers or seers who had a special relationship with the spiritual world, and who would assist in explaining and dealing with its vagaries. Hunting technology varied widely across the vast Middle North, as indigenous peoples developed the techniques and tools that best suited the particular harvestable resources in their area. The harvesting cycle rested very heavily on the work of women and children. There is a tendency to see aboriginal harvesting in male terms — hunting a moose or a caribou has often been of more interest to non-Natives than berry-picking, snaring gophers or drying fish. Women, however, played a vital role in the harvesting routine.

There is, consequently, no single indigenous culture in the Provincial Norths. Social, cultural, spiritual and harvesting patterns varied widely across the region. Inuit snow houses had little in common with Tsimshian longhouses; the sea-

oriented harvesting Inuit culture was different in many respects from the mobile existence of the Woodlands Cree. Similarly, Ojibwa spirituality was unique and special, as was that
of the Beaver and the Naskapi. It is too simplistic to suggest
that these different cultures emerged out of the particular ecological zones in which they lived, although they did take many
aspects of their character from their surroundings. To accept
this is to denigrate the importance of human agency, and to
adopt a level of "cultural materialism" — the line of analysis
by anthropologist Marvin Harris that suggests that culture
flows from biological considerations — that cloaks many important aspects of indigenous culture.

If the aboriginal peoples of the Middle North shared one
thing, it was their adaptability. The northern ecosystem was
such that it demanded flexibility and quick response to changing economic or human circumstances. If population exceeded
the level of safely harvested resources, the group had to dis-
band into smaller units or move en masse to a new location.
Animal cycles, climatic change, conflict with other indigenous
groups, and other shifts often demanded such a quick response. Because of the relative absence of material possessions,
sophisticated means of transportation, ability to live off the
land, and ease of constructing new shelters, these societies
possessed the cultural and material means to respond rapidly
to new realities. This flexibility would stand them in very good
stead in the years after contact with Europeans.

Leaving aside fanciful voyages by Irish monks, Welsh
princes, lost tribes of Israel, and other pretenders to the honour
(now increasingly tarnished) of being the first European in
North America, the first such contact probably occurred between the Norse (Vikings) and the indigenous people of Labrador, sometime around the end of the tenth century. But
there is no memory or evidence of this except for remains
found at L'Anse aux Meadows, at the northern tip of Newfoundland. A controversial argument first advanced by the
late T. Oleson suggested that the Inuit may have emerged out
of sexual and cultural unions of the Norse and the indigenous
peoples of the Labrador region. This analysis has been severely
criticized, and contradicts the preponderance of evidence
which suggests a west to east migration across the Arctic, and

not the reverse as Oleson suggests. More regular contact began around the year 1500, when Portuguese, Basque and British fishing boats began to land on the coast to dry the fish they had caught on the Grand Banks of Newfoundland. From the beginning, these fishermen brought goods to trade for furs, and soon the Native people began to congregate in the summer to meet them along the Gulf of St. Lawrence, although not in Newfoundland, where the Beothuk retreated in the face of conflict with the Europeans.

Before examining the historical pattern of contact, it is necessary to make a simple point. There is no single starting point for direct contact between indigenous peoples and newcomers. While the peoples in the far east of the continent encountered Europeans very early, and those of the Hudson Bay area had considerable experience with the newcomers by the seventeenth century, others in the interior did not have direct contact until almost a century later. Indigenous groups in the interior did, however, learn about the newcomers from other aboriginal peoples, and were typically well-prepared for them when the first European explorers finally arrived.

The inevitable result of early contact was that by the time Jacques Cartier arrived in the 1530s, and certainly long before Samuel de Champlain established the first permanent settlement in 1608, the Montagnais and Naskapis had suffered a loss of population. This was due to "virgin soil epidemics," one of the most important and devastating aspects of the European occupation of North America. The process was simple, and deadly. The Europeans brought with them many diseases to which the aboriginal peoples had no natural immunity. What might be a minor illness among the Europeans — chicken pox, measles, mumps or influenza — was likely to become a pandemic when visited upon the indigenous population. When smallpox, the greatest killer of indigenous peoples around the world, accompanied the Europeans, a large percentage of people they met were sure to die. The epidemics were not deliberately introduced, but they nonetheless had a terrible impact on the local peoples. In some areas, over half of the population perished within a few years; a single outbreak of smallpox, in a few cases, killed two-thirds of the people in a particular group.

Scholars can only guess at the demographic and cultural implications of these diseases. There were no census takers around in the early years, and many indigenous groups, hundreds of miles in the interior, felt the scourge of these diseases long before they saw the first European. The death of many elders — often the most vulnerable to illness — the inability of spiritual leaders to explain or control the epidemics, and the loss of hunters and leaders to the diseases and other consequences, caused many serious disruptions of indigenous cultures. While precision is impossible, there is little doubt that the introduction of virgin soil epidemics killed many people over the years; some groups lost more than 50 percent of their population. As American demographic historian Henry Dobyns has suggested, the land that Europeans entered in the era of settlement was not virgin territory, but widowed land.

While the contemporary tendency is to see the Middle North as marginal at best, in the early years of contact it was in fact the centre of European attempts to occupy and exploit the northern half of North America. The focus of newcomer activity was the fur trade, a relatively minor element in the European economy, but vital to the pattern of exploration and expansion in what is now Canada. While the administrators of New France made a few perfunctory efforts to develop agriculture along the St. Lawrence, they devoted most of their efforts to expanding trade into the lands north and west of their main settlements at Quebec (1608) and Montreal (1642). The Naskapi and Montagnais lost their position of prominence as competition with the British and Dutch forced the French to expand their trading activities to the west, but the Ojibwa, in particular, found themselves as the beneficiaries of the expanding fur trade activity.

Interest in the fur trade led in 1670 to the establishment of the British trading firm, the Company of Adventurers Trading into Hudson Bay, otherwise known as the Hudson's Bay Company. After focusing initially on the James Bay region, the HBC shifted its attention to the west shore of Hudson Bay, where the new posts of York Factory and Fort Churchill provided access to the vast trading lands of the Cree and Chipewyan. The French responded by moving westward, initially to the

Great Lakes region, where they competed for the James Bay trade, and later, in the 1730s, into the Lake Winnipeg area. Their successors, the Montreal traders, moved into what are now the Provincial Norths of Manitoba and Saskatchewan, where they established an intense rivalry with the HBC for the trading affections of the Natives of the interior.

The indigenous peoples responded enthusiastically to the opportunities thus presented. There was little hesitation in seeking the new material and technological resources available from the Hudson's Bay Company and its French rivals. But Native peoples were not, as was long believed, willing to give everything they possessed for these new items, nor were they guileless "savages" who were easily hoodwinked into un-favourable trading arrangements by the more clever Europeans. Instead, the Natives traded for those goods which they found useful or desirable — metal items, particularly knives, axes and pots, clothing, blankets, tobacco, and alcohol. But they quickly learned to leave behind inferior goods and those of marginal utility. Early on they became astute traders, economic partners of the Europeans in fact if not in name, happily prepared to play European competitors off against each other and willing to travel a long distance to secure a better deal.

Many changes accompanied the expansion of the fur trade, particularly among the Ojibwa and Cree, who adapted quickly to the new realities and moved large distances to remain in contact with the westward-shifting fur trade. They even moved into new territories, pushing aside less commercially-oriented groups. A number of bands, and here again the Cree and Ojibwa stand out, established themselves as guides, hunt-ers and intermediaries for the Hudson's Bay Company, the French traders and more distant Native bands. These new trading opportunities placed the intermediaries in a favourable trading position and ensured them some measure of influence over the structure and direction of the fur trade.

The Europeans, although surprised by the Natives' ability to control aspects of the trade, had their own commercial agenda, influenced for a period by international rivalries be-tween the French and British (and in northwest British Colum-bia, between the British, Americans and Russians). The French and British rivalry eventually reached from north of the St. Lawrence to northern Saskatchewan. The British conquest of New France in 1759–60, ratified by treaty in 1763, seemingly gave the Hudson's Bay Company a complete monopoly, as spelled out in its 1670 charter. But competing traders, in this case an unusual amalgamation of British, American and French traders, took over the Montreal-based fur trade empire, and quickly expanded westward to challenge the more conservative Hudson's Bay Company. The Montreal traders eventually came together as the North West Company and created an aggressive, competitive organization that soon expanded as far north as the Mackenzie River valley and as far west as the Columbia River and the Pacific Coast. The Hudson's Bay Company responded more cautiously, moving first to Cumberland House in 1774 and then slowly into the interior, establishing an intense struggle for the trade, particularly in the rich Athabasca district.

The resulting competition inflicted considerable hardship on the indigenous peoples. The rival firms, particularly the Montrealers, adopted alcohol as a primary means of attracting Native traders, thus introducing a disruptive element into their society. Similarly, the commercial rivalry introduced a level of competition and violence never before experienced in the region, leading to struggles between and within indigenous groups, and encouraging conflict over traditional territories and harvestable resources. In key zones, particularly northern Manitoba, fur resources were steadily depleted, to the point that the area became virtually useless for trading purposes.

Extensive trading networks developed across the Middle North as the two fur empires struck out westward. The Hudson's Bay Company's operations, based on the port at York Factory, the interior entrepôt at Norway House and the increasingly important centre at Fort Garry and Red River, were costly and not always effective. The North West Company expanded more aggressively, based on Peter Pond's identification of the Methy Portage in 1779, which provided access to the vital Athabasca district. From there, the NWC moved further west, following Alexander Mackenzie's (1793) and Simon Fraser's (1805–07) paths beyond the Rocky Mountains and establishing posts at Fort St. John and Fort George in the newly identified region.

The rivalry continued to the point of mutual exhaustion. The North West Company and the Hudson's Bay Company drove each other to the brink of bankruptcy, a situation complicated by embarrassment in Britain over the increasing violence and conflict in Rupert's Land. The situation culminated in the 1821 merger of the Hudson's Bay Company and the North West Company and the subsequent reorganization of the fur trade under the firm hand of Governor George Simpson. The new measures caused much hardship across the Middle North, as posts were closed, workers laid off, and strict conservation measures were implemented in areas that had been over-hunted during the period of intense competition.

The new fur trade continued many of the patterns of the past, albeit on a reduced and less dramatic basis. Competitive traders, including American rivals and free traders based in British North America, ensured that some level of rivalry remained in place, but at a much-reduced scale from the halcyon days of HBC–NWC conflict. The indigenous peoples, who had adapted rapidly and successfully to the early fur trade, suffered with its decline. Alice Kehoe offers a useful summary of the impact of the post-1821 trade on the Ojibwa:

> After the merger, the Bay used its monopoly position to enforce unprecedented economies, including a virtual end to the "gifts" through which traders gave Indians better value for their furs ... Most unfortunately, not only were beaver and other fur bearers fewer in number after well over a century of intensified trapping, but moose and caribou were much fewer. In many sectors, no large game was normally seen ... for the rest of the nineteenth century and into the early twentieth century, the northern Ojibway and adjacent boreal-forest Cree lived principally on fish and hares, the dull famine relief of happier times ... Poorer nutrition made the Indians more susceptible to infections and less able to recover quickly from wounds or accidents. It became more difficult, too, to keep warm when moose and especially caribou hides could no longer be obtained in needed quantities ... the people had to

substitute shirts and coats of rabbit skin cut into strips, twisted as into thread, and woven into a fur fabric. (Whole rabbit skins are thin, and too flimsy for boreal-forest winter clothing ...) There are indications in the traders' records that crises of leadership and perhaps faith occurred ... It must have seemed that spirit helpers had deserted the people.

The fur traders did not come alone, for true to their European origins, they brought their spiritual conventions, assumptions and institutions with them. Church of England clerics followed the Hudson's Bay Company to Red River (1820) and to several of the larger trading posts; Roman Catholic priests and nuns accompanied the French fur traders into the West, and established a denominational rivalry for the souls and loyalty of the Natives in the region. The Catholics had freer reign in eastern districts, particularly among the Naskapi and Montagnais. Other Christian proselytizers, including the Moravians among the Inuit and Innu of Labrador (1752 and 1771), and the Church Missionary Society, led by the controversial William Duncan, among the Tsimshian of Metlakatla (founded 1887), sought out spiritual niches, anxious to spread the good word and "save" the indigenous people from their age-old barbarism and savagery. In many cases the Natives responded positively; many became practising Christians and seemed to have adopted the social, if not the spiritual, values of the missionaries. Often, however, they adopted Christianity as part of a spiritual system which remained Native at the core.

The fur trade era reoriented life in the Middle North, introducing the commercialization of fur-bearing resources and drawing the indigenous peoples into the capitalist economy. The effect of the fur trade on the indigenous people of North America has been hotly debated, not the least because it has sometimes served as a metaphor for modern aboriginal grievances. There are two important truths about the fur trade and indigenous peoples: first, most welcomed the advance of the trade, and second, for most of the time they had a greater degree of control over it than is popularly supposed. This is not necessarily to say that the trade was a "good thing" for the indigenous people; it brought the devastation of disease, over-hunting of game, the introduction of alcohol, and considerable social change, some of it for the worse. But the indigenous people often welcomed the technology and material advances that the traders had to offer. Iron and steel knives, axes, pots, and other material goods were perceived as useful and an improvement on traditional tools. They were consequently adopted across the region; old technology and the knowledge of how to make and use the old tools such as the bow and arrow soon fell by the wayside. Nor could the indigenous traders be fobbed off with inferior goods; they knew the difference between good and poor quality, and knew the appropriate price for what they wanted. It is true that over time this pattern of purchases bound the aboriginal peoples to the European trading system; iron goods, at first labour-saving devices, became essentials. But this process is certainly not evidence of some character flaw unique to the indigenous peoples, nor a sign of their inability to make the "correct" decisions, as any North American who has tried living without electricity and the internal combustion engine might agree.

The economic consequences were also momentous. In some respects, the trade simply brought new goods into an existing commercial and trading system. For instance, there have always been Native intermediaries involved with exchange, as people passed goods along from one group to another, sometimes over distances that seem surprising, as when articles from the Gulf of Mexico such as shell ornaments show up in northwestern Ontario, for example. Nevertheless, the fact that the indigenous peoples were now tied to distant market economies over which they ultimately had no control inevitably meant that they enjoyed less influence over their destiny than before. Fundamental changes occurred over the decades, as indigenous peoples from Labrador to northern British Columbia became increasingly tied to the capitalist economy. The Hudson's Bay Company, which always had a long view of its business, made it a practice to extend credit to its Native trading partners when prices were low or game stocks depleted. While a humane gesture, this policy was fundamentally commercial, for it tied the indigenous people into the Company-based economic system. As historian A. J. Ray pointed out,

The arrangement discouraged, and often prevented, Indians from leaving this part of the primary resource sector of the economy, even in regions where resources were so depleted that only marginal livelihoods could be sustained ... the HBC was partly responsible for limiting the ability of Indians to adjust to new economic circumstances at the beginning of this century. Debt-ridden, repeatedly blocked from alternative opportunities for over a century, and accustomed to various forms of relief over two centuries, Indians became so evidently demoralized in this century, but the groundwork for this was laid in the more distant past.

Without unduly romanticizing the life of the First Nations in the Provincial Norths before the 1870s, it is possible to argue that the assault on their way of life brought by the fur trade economy was much less disruptive than the mining, industrial, and bureaucratic invasions that would follow. Whether or not the fur trade is viewed as exploitive, it at least was based on activities central to indigenous life — hunting, trapping and travelling. When the indigenous peoples of northern Manitoba, for example, began to hunt for game to sell to the traders at Fort Churchill and York Factory, instead of simply hunting for their own food, this was but an extension of a traditional way of life. A. J. Ray has argued, however, that even in this early period one can see the origins of more institutionalized dependency; the Hudson's Bay Company's use of credit to bind Native traders to the trade, even in regions where depleted resources permitted them only a marginal commercial existence, was at least partially responsible for limiting the options and ability of the indigenous people to adjust to new economic circumstances.

As late as 1870, as the Hudson's Bay Company gradually lost control of the southern fur trade, the Middle North remained the preserve of the old order. The changes outlined above — greater use of credit, conservation measures, the continued dislocations associated with epidemic diseases, the confusion and reorientation associated with the arrival of the missionaries — had considerable impact, but the fur trade economy remained vital and important. The prerogatives of European expansion, particularly those of the agricultural, logging and mining frontiers, had not yet moved aggressively into the region. Many historians have, somewhat inaccurately, assumed that the HBC's surrender of its monopoly over Rupert's Land in 1870 marked a major turning point across the country. This is simply not true for the Provincial Norths, where the social and economic structures of the past remained relatively intact.

Changes were in the offing, however. Until 1870, the Middle North attracted little attention outside of fur trade circles. Characterizations of the region emphasized the cold, ice and snow, and the unattractiveness of the land for European settlement. The creation of the new Dominion of Canada in 1867, and the country's imperialistic dream of territorial expansion, created new expectations for the unsettled districts, and fueled enthusiastic, but unrealistic, expectations for the North. Until the 1870s, the British government had generally left the region to the fur traders, particularly the Hudson's Bay Company, and had made few efforts to assert European-style sovereignty over the vast land. The Robinson-Huron and Robinson-Superior Treaties of the 1850s in Upper Canada/Canada West did draw some indigenous peoples into a more complex relationship with European authorities, but the rest of the aboriginal inhabitants of the Middle North had little direct contact with newcomer administrators or officials.

Confederation and the subsequent extension of administrative control over what are now the Provincial Norths would bring sweeping changes to the region. Age-old patterns of occupation, resource use and social organization had been uprooted over the previous two centuries by the advance of the fur trade. The indigenous inhabitants of the area responded to the changes, showing the flexibility that had been so central to their adaptation to the sub-Arctic regions. For the North and its peoples, now including a smattering of non-indigenous peoples, most of them in the region temporarily to work with the aboriginal residents, greater changes lay ahead. The next task for the newcomers, dictated by the creation of Canada and the gradual establishment of new provincial jurisdictions across the country, was to draw political boundaries across this immense territory.

Chapter Two

The Incorporation of Northern Regions

Canadians, unlike people who live in parts of the world where political boundaries tend to be fluid, usually take the permanence of theirs for granted. Our provincial boundaries especially are widely accepted as legitimate, logical, and historically correct. There are exceptions, such as Quebec's challenge to Newfoundland's control of Labrador, but most Canadians assume that the status quo has an historical and regional integrity that makes it unassailable. Whether or not this is true for southern Canada — and the separatist impulses of French-speaking peoples in Quebec, New Brunswick and Ontario makes it clear that political boundaries do not necessarily follow cultural or linguistic groupings, nor are boundaries or nations themselves unchangeable — it certainly does not apply as easily in the northern realm, where the provinces of Canada for years have argued for, and over, the northward extension of their territorial control.

There was a particular logic to this battle for northern territories. In the early years after Confederation, the North represented a kind of provincial *lebensraum* to provincial politicians: space to grow, and potential resources for the expansion and enrichment of the southern economy. Northern areas, though not likely to be suitable for agriculture, held great promise for future development and were consequently very much worth fighting over. Almost from the time of Confederation, therefore, those provincial premiers with a geographic northland began to demand a northward extension of their boundaries, requesting specifically that the federal government relinquish control of portions of its vast northern territories, ceding portions of the Northwest Territories to the provinces.

Canadians seem prone to a peculiar national malady best described as "mappism" — an infatuation with the size of this country combined with a disinclination to visit or learn anything about its more remote regions. But they often forget that this country began as a small collection of southerly colonies: Nova Scotia, New Brunswick, Quebec and Ontario, the first two without northern regions, and the norths of the latter two restricted to relatively small bands of land north of the Saint Lawrence River system. In 1867 the British government still maintained formal (though in practice barely actual) control of much of what is now Canada, in particular northern Ontario, northern Quebec, all of what are now the Prairie provinces, the Yukon and the Northwest Territories. British authorities were anxious to surrender their responsibilities for these enormous, sparsely populated tracts of land and, in 1869–1870, arranged for the transfer of the enormous Hudson's Bay Company holdings, then described as the North-West Territories, to Canada.

British Columbia, the first province to join the new country, entered Confederation with its jurisdiction over northern lands already established. The colony of British Columbia came into being in 1858 as a response to the discovery of gold in the Fraser River valley. Anxious to assert control over the incoming flood of prospectors, and believing (correctly, it was soon proven) that even richer gold deposits lay further north, the British government established the new colony with a northern boundary running along the Finlay River (at about 56°N). When further discoveries were made in the Stikine country, London in 1863 gave the colony of British Columbia administrative responsibility for the Stickeen (Stikine) Territory. The northern boundary for this territory was initially set at 62°, a line which would have attached the southern Yukon to the province, but which was later reduced, for no particularly obvious reason, to 60°. When British Columbia joined Confederation in 1871, it did so as a reluctant bride, with its northern boundary set, and with its northeastern boundary shifted from its initial line — 125° west (just west of the modern community of Fraser Lake) — to its permanent location at 120° west. British Columbia, alone among the early partners in the Canadian experiment, entered with a northern hinterland already in place.

Ironically, the last British colony to enter Confederation also did so with its claim to northern lands firmly established. Newfoundland, destined to remain a separate British colony until 1949, had long-standing claims to the control of the Labrador coast as well as an indeterminate amount of territory inland of it. Although the French and British had long argued over formal control of the area, the region's limited commercial and settlement prospects meant that no one cared much where the western boundary of Labrador ran. The matter assumed new urgency in the early twentieth century, when the extension of the timber industry into Labrador brought Newfoundland's claims to the land into direct competition with Quebec's aspirations in the area. Quebec's position, championed by Canada and hotly contested by the Newfoundland government, was that the island dominion's legitimate rights applied only to the coast and did not extend into the interior. After extended political and legal debate which went as far as the Judicial Committee of the Privy Council in London, the matter was settled in 1927 in Newfoundland's favour: Labrador would be defined as those lands draining into the north Atlantic and demarcated by the height of land, rather than the narrow coastal strip Canada had been willing to grant. Quebec resisted the decision, and remains unhappy with it. The province's northern and northeastern boundaries are in fact not entirely settled, at least not in the minds of separatists, who dream of a unilateral repudiation of the Privy Council decision. Some federalists, on the other hand, are at pains to point out that much of Quebec's Provincial North was not part of New France or of pre-Confederation Quebec, nor has the province any long-standing historical right to it; it was a gift of the federal government in this century.

Nova Scotia and New Brunswick had no contiguous northern territories to claim or aspire to, but for Ontario and Quebec, the two original Canadian provinces with northern ambitions, wresting control of additional lands proved to be a long and difficult process. From the early years of Confederation, Ontario and Quebec were determined to extend their political grasp northward and gain control of as much as possible of the vast zones designated on the early maps of Canada as the North-West Territories.

For Ontario, the matter of a boundary to the north and west became particularly pressing with Canada's purchase of Rupert's Land in 1869–1870. The provincial government had, from the years preceding Confederation, exercised *de facto* jurisdiction over the region west of Lake Superior. Not surprisingly, Ontario wanted its control over these lands confirmed through the establishment of formal boundaries. Lengthy battles ensued, often lost in arcane legal debates, but at other times boiling over into federal-provincial confrontations. For Manitoba and Ontario, the struggle was far from trivial, for the rich forest lands and potential mineral deposits of the Lake of the Woods region lay in the contested area. The matter was finally settled in 1884, once more by the Judicial Committee of the Privy Council, with the boundary favouring Ontario and running north along 95° west. The resolution of the Ontario-Manitoba boundary set a northwest limit for the province of Ontario, and re-defined the province's northern boundary, establishing a line which ran along a convoluted network of rivers from the upper reaches of the Lake of the Woods to the outflow of the Albany River on James Bay. Ontario's northward extension was substantially, although not totally, complete.

Quebec, like Ontario, had northern ambitions. Initially, debate focused on the province's argument that the original northern boundary had been drawn too far to the south, and that Quebec had a legitimate claim to lands further north. While the Canadian government generally agreed with this position, long discussions ensued about the appropriate boundary line. The matter was resolved in 1898, resulting in the establishment of a new northern boundary that ran roughly along the Eastmain River and the 53° N latitude. This, for a time, answered Quebec's territorial ambitions in the North. When early in the twentieth century the Canadian government began to carve up the vast holdings purchased from the Hudson's Bay Company, both Ontario and Quebec were quick to press new demands for additional northern lands.

A further division of Canada's territorial holdings began on the western plains. Manitoba, initially a postage-stamp-sized province in the Red River valley, lobbied incessantly for additional land. As settlers pressed westward and occupied the rich agricultural lands of the southern and central Canadian prairie, demands arose for the establishment of new political jurisdictions in the region. Manitoba's pleas were answered in stages, as the boundary was extended north, west and east in 1881 (the eastern portions, from Lake of the Woods to Port Arthur, were transferred to Ontario in the Privy Council decision of 1884). The settled lands were initially organized into a series of administrative districts — Keewatin, Athabasca, Alberta, Saskatchewan and Assiniboia — with the areas as yet without significant non-Native populations remaining within the North-West Territories. The boundaries of these internal, territorial districts were redrawn on several occasions, and new jurisdictions — the District of Ungava and Mackenzie — were added. These divisions, designed to answer local demands for greater attention from government, were anything but permanent.

Pressure from within these newly colonized territories, particularly among the farmers of the western plains, combined with demands from the provinces of Manitoba, Ontario and Quebec for additions to their land holdings, led to a substantial redrafting of the internal map of Canada in the first two decades of the twentieth century. Promoters and politicians advanced a variety of ideas for the restructuring of the map of Western Canada, in particular advocating everything from the enlargement of Manitoba to the west to the creation of two new Prairie provinces, one for the northern sections and one for the south.

In determining the future political shape of Western Canada, the federal government of Liberal prime minister Wilfrid Laurier made a series of decisions which did more than anything else to shape the boundaries of the modern Provincial Norths. For reasons that had more to do with the prevailing indifference towards Canada's North than to any specific geographic knowledge of the region, the government decided that the lands north of 60° would remain as territories; in an era of preoccupation with agricultural settlement, the assumption that commercial agriculture could not flourish north of that line placed a seemingly permanent brake on Arctic prospects. The government also decided that the suggestion that everything between British Columbia and Manitoba be made into one giant province was impractical; there would have to be two new Prairie provinces, but they would be given their own northern hinterlands. To balance the map, and to make the new provinces equal with British Columbia, the sixtieth parallel became the northern limit for boundaries across the prairies.

Thus it was in the first years of the twentieth century, those years which Wilfrid Laurier prophesied would be the "century of Canada," that the province-making exercise began in earnest. After much debate, Alberta and Saskatchewan entered Confederation in 1905; like Manitoba, they came in as second-class provinces, without control over provincial lands and natural resources. There was much criticism of the location of their mutual boundary, but little discussion of northern reaches of the provinces. These lands, unevenly developed and poorly known, had few non-Native residents and had attracted little attention; however, they did offer Alberta and Saskatchewan some assurance of future growth. But until 1930, when Ottawa relinquished control over Crown lands in the Prairie provinces, their sovereignty over their Provincial Norths was largely nominal.

Granting two western provinces northern hinterlands — matched by British Columbia, which likewise extended to the sixtieth parallel — raised the ante across the country. Manitoba, Ontario and Quebec cast covetous eyes at the old fur trading districts to the far north, and demanded that the federal government redraw their boundaries to give them real Provincial Norths as well. Saskatchewan complicated matters by asking for the band of land in between the existing northern boundary of Manitoba and the sixtieth parallel, claiming that it required this territory for an outlet to the sea and, moreover, had a natural and historical relationship with the area. Manitoba countered this claim, which would have put the future port of Churchill in Saskatchewan, with a request for the extension of its boundary to the sixtieth parallel and Hudson Bay, arguing that it was best suited to govern the sparsely populated area.

The claims by Ontario and Quebec were similarly based on a combination of historical right, economic aspiration and political convenience. Ontario generally supported Manitoba's claim for a northward extension, but also wanted its boundary to extend to Hudson Bay, thus incorporating sizeable new territories. Quebec also grasped at more land, declaring its interest in the areas extending north from its boundary to Hudson Strait.

As had been the case earlier, the southern provinces were preoccupied with considerations of size, economic potential, and prestige. The now hotly debated Mid-North offered the provinces all three, and promised to finish the long-standing discussion over the internal boundaries of the country. The federal government, for its part, was not unwilling to surrender its direct administrative responsibility for these northern lands, most of which were loosely governed through detachments of the North West Mounted Police and by arrangements with missionaries and traders. Boundary extension seemed to be the answer to all the participants' dreams. Since the Native people who inhabited these lands were not enfranchised, and were considered unlikely to have useful opinions on such matters of state, they were simply not consulted on decisions that would ultimately have a profound effect on their lives.

Faced with competing interests and the prospects of extensive inter-provincial squabbling, the federal government considered a number of alternatives. According to Norman Nicholson, the leading scholar of Canadian boundaries,

> It appears that the government of Canada gave consideration to the creation of entirely new provinces out of the areas lying north of Manitoba, Ontario, and Quebec but concluded that climatic conditions were such that new provinces could not be created. "If then, that territory cannot be turned into new provinces, does it not seem the best way to deal with it is to annex it to the existing provinces?"

After much consideration and negotiation, the provinces got what they requested, except for Saskatchewan, which had to be content with growing north rather than north and northeast.

Under the new arrangements, negotiated during the years of Liberal rule but implemented in 1912 by the Conservative government of Robert Borden, Manitoba, Ontario and Quebec saw their territories extended northward. The Manitoba-Ontario border, proposed by Ontario to meet Hudson Bay at the mouth of the Churchill River, was moved far to the east, joining salt water at the eighty-ninth meridian. Quebec received most of what it requested, with the northern limits being extended to Hudson Strait, thus incorporating the vast northern peninsula, though the prize of Labrador was to elude it. Quebec had also hoped to gain control of a series of islands in Hudson Bay and Hudson Strait; that request, like those of the other provinces wishing northern islands, was turned down by the federal government.

As of 1912, therefore, the present provincial boundaries of Canada had been drawn (excluding those of Newfoundland until 1949). Most of the provinces now had a potential northern hinterland, having gained control of vast territories. British Columbia brought northern territories with it into Confederation. Quebec, Ontario and Manitoba extended the northern limits to their lands only through extensive discussions with neighbouring provinces and the federal government. Alberta and Saskatchewan, twentieth-century creations of the nation state, perhaps represented the quintessential Canadian province, with large southern agricultural areas, and vast tracts of land in the Middle North, containing untold and unknown mineral resources, rich carpets of potentially marketable timber, and holding the prospect for future provincial growth and development.

Because these lines have existed on maps for eighty years, there is a tendency to assume that the provincial boundaries, created out of circumstances of flux, political debate and extended negotiation, are the logical internal boundaries for Canada. Yet there is ample evidence that the incorporation of northern lands into a collection of southern-oriented provinces was neither culturally, geographically, economically or even historically logical; certainly no attention was paid to the long-standing territorial boundaries observed by First Nations people. There was, for instance, a certain legitimacy to Saskatchewan's claim to an eastern outlet at Hudson Bay, which would have maintained the integrity of well-established connections with what is now northern Manitoba. Northern

British Columbia had only tenuous links with the southern portions of the province; the agricultural districts in the Peace River valley, for example, had retained long-standing connections with the contiguous zones of Alberta. The James Bay regions of Ontario and Quebec historically had only faint ties with the southern parts of the provinces, since their historical commercial link with the rest of the world ran through Hudson Bay rather than south to the St. Lawrence.

The lack of historical connections between north and south did not deter the provincial promoters and politicians who argued for the northern extension of the boundaries. Even though the regions were little-known, the promoters were nonetheless brimming with enthusiastic visions of economic opportunity and territorial grandeur. The North, they argued, held the raw materials necessary for industrial development and economic prosperity — even if no one knew exactly where they were. In a manner strikingly reminiscent of European colonizers and their attitudes toward overseas colonies, the southern districts looked upon the North as a permanent, well-controlled hinterland, to be developed in the interests of the broader political jurisdictions rather than those of the local population. This final period of provincial expansion also had the effect of drawing a neat line — the sixtieth parallel — between the usable land in Canada and that which was un-wanted. As a result, this arbitrary division between "north" and "south" has become fixed in the Canadian mind, with the sixtieth parallel somehow delineating the beginning of the "real" North, and turning the Provincial Norths — the equally northern districts immediately south of the line — into a sort of nowhere-land. This meant, as well, that the Yukon and Northwest Territories were defined simply as unwanted lands, regions beyond the limit of reasonable expectations of profit and return to the southern provinces, and hence best left as a permanent charge on the federal government.

Superficially, this process of territorial expansion suggested that the northern areas incorporated into the provinces were desirable regions, highly sought after by the provincial administrations. But, as subsequent chapters will reveal, this was not the case. The provinces did not want these districts because they had immediate plans for development, or because they had any interest in the people who lived in their remote and widely-scattered communities. Southerners saw the Provincial Norths as regions of the future, lands of promise and long-term opportunity; also, like children at a party, they sought to gain at the expense of others, to get more because someone else had received more, and to thus ensure that the neighbouring province did not receive an undue share of a potentially rich land.

It is important also to note that the redrafting of boundaries undertaken between 1867 and 1912 (plus the resolution of the question of the Labrador-Quebec boundary in 1927) did not end the question of northward expansion of the provinces. From time to time, in ways formal or subtle, more than one of the provinces has cast covetous eyes at Canada's remaining northern territories. The discovery of Klondike riches in the Yukon River basin in 1896 and of oil in the Mackenzie River valley in 1920 alerted several provinces to the prospects for a further expansion of their colonial empires. A quick glance at the current map reveals that nothing came of these deliberations; it does not, however, detract from the importance of these episodes in revealing southern attitudes toward territorial expansion.

The most serious challenge to the integrity of the post-1912 map of Canada came in the mid-1930s, when T. "Duff" Pattullo, a former Yukon resident, Prince Rupert booster and Liberal premier of British Columbia, proposed the annexation of the Yukon Territory. Pattullo was convinced that the future of his province, then mired in the Great Depression, lay in the North. The construction of a road to Alaska would, he argued, spark an immediate economic boom in northern British Columbia which would reverberate throughout the province, bringing general prosperity to the region and, more specifically, to the heavily populated south. A central element in this northern vision was British Columbia's acquisition of the Yukon Territory.

Yukoners voiced loud objections. As the Dawson City Board of Trade reported, "The miners, large and small, the trappers, the merchants, and the general body of the inhabitants of the Yukon are irreconcilably opposed to the annexation, which if carried out would convert the present contented and optimistic outlook of the people into one of discouragement, resentment and bitterness." Pattullo pressed on nevertheless. Prime Minister William Lyon Mackenzie King, a cautious man struggling with the economic and political consequences of a continent-wide depression, initially greeted Pattullo's proposal with some enthusiasm; it promised, after all, to free the federal government from an unwanted financial and administrative obligation. Pattullo's plan seemed assured of success in 1937, only to collapse at the final hour due to the resurrection of the decades-old Canadian debate about government funding for Roman Catholic schools. The Yukon supported one such school; British Columbia did not fund church-based institutions; the thought of a quarrel over denominational schools made Mackenzie King nervous, and he withdrew his support from the plan. For this seemingly trivial reason, the annexation scheme was abandoned, although British Columbia's dream of an expanded northern empire would never entirely disappear.

Alberta pushed a similar line in the 1930s, suggesting (although not as systematically as Pattullo and British Columbia had done) that the Mackenzie River valley be brought under its jurisdiction. In this instance, even more so than with the Yukon, the proposal carried considerable economic and cultural logic, for northern Alberta was closely connected with the region north of sixty. On occasion northerners advanced ideas of their own. In 1939, the Peace River Chamber of Commerce proposed that a new political jurisdiction — potentially a province — be established in the northwest, incorporating the Yukon Territory, Mackenzie River valley and the Peace River country. This suggested recasting of the provincial boundaries — this time proposed by people in the region rather than those on the outside — found little favour in Ottawa or the provincial capitals and disappeared without serious debate.

Dreams of provincial expansion, while primarily a product of the heady years of the late nineteenth and early twentieth century, did not disappear. In the 1960s, British Columbia premier W. A. C. Bennett loudly and repeatedly touted his "Five Regions" vision of Canada. Bennett's proposal called for the redrawing of provincial boundaries in such a way as to unify economically and culturally contiguous regions and to integrate the northern territories into the provinces. Under Bennett's scheme, British Columbia would gain control of the Yukon Territory, completing an age old dream of provincial expansion; the new Prairie province would take over much of Northwest Territories; and the eastern Arctic would be transferred to Ontario's control. The Maritime region, now including Newfoundland, Nova Scotia, New Brunswick and Prince Edward Island, would share a common northland — Labrador. W. A. C. Bennett's plan — like many of his ideas — generated considerable discussion and anger, but nothing came of it. The boundaries stayed intact, but at least one of the provinces had provided solid evidence that the age of territorial expansion was not yet over.

In more recent times, the question of northward expansion by the provinces has been given little public airing. Debate, in fact, has shifted to the equally contentious question of granting provincial status to the existing territories (although it is important to note that the Yukon and Northwest Territories are in no way committed to the idea), devolution of province-like powers from the federal to the territorial governments, and, more recently, the formal steps towards the creation of a third territory, Nunavut, out of the Northwest Territories.

On a more subtle level, however, there is evidence that the vision of further incorporation of northern territories has not yet died. The failure of the Meech Lake Accord, for example, provided some revealing hints about provincial attitudes to the North. The provincial premiers, in what northerners felt was a humiliating and anti-democratic act, rejected territorial appeals that they be treated equitably in the redrafting of the constitution. Territorial rights received virtually no consideration from the would-be fathers of a new Confederation, who blithely ignored the political rights of the Yukon and Northwest Territories.

While there have been a variety of interpretations offered for this assault on territorial rights, more than one careful observer of the constitutional process has attributed it to the fact that several provinces have unresolved territorial ambitions in the Canadian North. It is their hope, the argument goes, that future political negotiations will result in another northward extension of certain provincial boundaries. Southern Canada's northern vision, as expressed through the further incorporation of territorial lands by the provinces, may well be still alive — although rarely expressed openly.

Despite the continued provincial claims and ambitions, the map of the Provincial Norths (excepting Newfoundland) was basically set by 1912. This process occurred without any consultation with people living in the former territories; the opinions of Native people were not valued at all, and the few non-Natives in the areas were largely agents of southern interests — fur trading, mining and lumber companies, or the federal government. Without a voice in its own future, the Mid-North was simply carved up by federal and provincial officials according to their own agenda, needs and interests.

Thus the framework for the development and non-Native settlement of the Provincial Norths had been established by the second decade of the twentieth century. There was now a vast northern empire waiting to be exploited. But not all provinces approached this task with equal zeal. The three Prairie provinces lacked control of their land and natural resources, and therefore were without the powers necessary to capitalize properly on northern opportunities. Newfoundland, not yet in Confederation and struggling with internal difficulties, scarcely gave much consideration to Labrador, except when its sovereignty over the region was challenged. In British Columbia, Ontario and Quebec, the provincial governments had the political will and economic muscle to permit and encourage the preliminary development of their northern districts. There would be, therefore, no single pattern of development and settlement in the Provincial Norths; as internal colonies, these regions were beholden to their political masters. It would be the southern, metropolitan districts of the provinces, not the northern regions, nor even the nation, that would set the primary agenda for regional growth, development and change. It is to these processes, and the manner in which the vast tracts of sub-Arctic and Arctic lands were incorporated within provincial boundaries, that this study now turns.

Chapter Three

The Colonizers' North

The debate over the political boundaries of the Canadian North hid more fundamental aspirations. Provincial governments from St. John's to Victoria believed that the northern reaches of their provinces represented the future of their respective corners of Confederation. In some instances, such as in Quebec, where the Provincial North gradually became an outlet for nationalist aspirations, the provinces had the sense that the newly acquired land represented an immediate opportunity for its citizens and businesses. More often, however, the acquisition of northern territories was thought of as a long-term investment; only in later years, as the resource potential of the region became more widely known, would the provinces look northward with excitement and urgency rather than mere acquisitiveness.

There would be no simple unfolding of the frontier of development and settlement in the Provincial Norths. The standard conception of the frontier is as a slowly advancing line of non-indigenous settlers, each stage building on the work and determination of the one that preceded it. This pattern — if it ever worked in this simple fashion anywhere across the continent — does not properly explain the development of the Provincial Norths. There are a few areas — the small agricultural regions in northern Quebec, northern Ontario and the Peace River country — that were "opened," to use that Eurocentric conception, following the occupation of agricultural regions to the south of them. But perhaps the best way of picturing northern development is to think of it as "island hopping," a process by which non-Natives discovered and exploited small disparate pockets of resources. Rather than a solid, steadily advancing line of settlement, the Provincial Norths experienced the opening of an isolated mine, the

development of a narrow railway corridor, a pocket of agriculture, a timber operation and other islands of non-indigenous occupation. Cole Harris, an historical geographer,
once described Canada as an archipelago; following this line,
the Provincial Norths between 1867 and 1945 represented the
fringe of islands at the extreme edge of the archipelago.

The first post–fur trade non-Native settlements in the Provincial Norths were established by miners. In the west, prospectors following the promise of massive deposits of gold
pushed north from California in the 1850s. The British Columbia gold rush began in the lower Fraser River valley in 1858
but soon pushed northward into the Cariboo district. The Cariboo gold rush, centred on the boomtown of Barkerville (1862),
resulted in the development of several promising gold fields
and the construction of the Cariboo Road (1862–65), which
provided a costly but vital transportation artery into the northern interior and which almost bankrupted the colonial government. But the glittering promise of northern British Columbia
soon faded. The gold prospectors pushed on into the Stikine
and Cassiar River country in the 1870s, sparking short-lived
booms in both areas. The miners pressed ever northward into
the Yukon River valley, culminating in the world famous
Klondike gold rush of 1897–1899. Northern British Columbia
slipped from view as the focus of attention shifted into the
Territorial North, but the small string of communities created
by the gold rush — Telegraph Creek, Dease Lake, Lower Post
— remained. The earlier mining and service communities,
along with new ones like Cassiar, overlaying the existing network of trading posts, provided the foundation for settlement
in the northern interior.

Northern British Columbia continued to attract some attention from the miners, and in the decades after the Cariboo
rush, prospectors continued to scour the valleys and hillsides,
hoping to strike it rich and start another development boom.
The mining companies, however, had their hands full with the
rich mineral properties in the southern parts of the province.
Northern transportation costs, particularly given the absence
of a suitable network, mitigated against any major development. The prospectors persisted, however, and properties,
particularly gold deposits, were developed where feasible. But

the large-scale, permanent developments that many had hoped would follow the Cariboo gold rush simply did not occur. A rush to the Dease Lake district in 1925 which attracted over 100 prospectors was not sustainable, and only three or four men made even moderate returns.

Perhaps the most dramatic mining activity, certainly the most sustained to occur in the Provincial Norths in the post-Confederation period, took place in northern Ontario, though there was a great deal of mining development in northern Quebec as well. Scientists working for the Geological Survey of Canada had long believed that the Canadian Shield country of northern Ontario and Quebec contained rich mineral deposits, and Ontario passed acts in 1868 and 1869 to regulate mining. The first discovery of important minerals came by accident in 1883, during the construction of the Canadian Pacific Railway near Sudbury. Mining of copper and nickel began in 1886, and Sudbury soon became the largest nickel producer in the world; by 1890 iron ore production was 190,000 tons. Morris Zaslow's description of early mining activity shows that environmental pollution was present from the start:

> The ore was roasted in the open on vast piles of wood to reduce the sulphur content and produce a rich copper-nickel matte which was exported mainly to the United States for refining. In the process the trees were cut down for miles about, while the sulphur and arsenic fumes poisoned the vegetation over a still wider area.

An important though short-lived discovery of rich silver ore occurred on a tiny island, only eighty feet in diameter, in Lake Superior near Thunder Bay; over $3 million worth of ore was taken from it in the late 1880s. A more long-lasting mining operation was begun by a chance discovery. The Northern Ontario Railway, chartered in 1902, was a provincially funded line designed to open the region of the province north of North Bay and to establish a provincial link to salt water at James Bay. The unexpected discovery of silver deposits near Lake Timiskaming during the railway's construction in 1903 led to the founding of the town of Cobalt, and within a year the railway was actually making a profit for the government.

The Cobalt field was a highly profitable one, producing over $17 million by 1912, and it spurred prospectors to look for other deposits in the region. The hopes of regional boosters for further development were soon realized. In 1909 gold was discovered at Timmins, and in 1912 at Kirkland Lake, and the railway was extended to both locations; by 1920 Ontario was becoming a major producer of gold (in 1983, Ontario produced $363 million of Canada's $1.2 billion worth of gold). The mining activity also had a strong effect on the economy of Ontario, perhaps the first time that a Provincial North had achieved such prominence in a provincial economy. Stockbrokers in Toronto and elsewhere, the *Northern Miner* — the journal of the industry — the growth of university departments of mining and geology, the royalties which rolled into the provincial coffers: all bore witness to this prominence. Of course, for every winner in the mining game there were many more losers. An Ontario commission reported in 1955 that of the approximately 4,000 gold mining companies that had been incorporated in the province to that date, only about 35 had returned sufficient dividends to cover the cost of bringing them into production.

The Provincial North of Quebec in the same period was undergoing a development of its forestry more than its mining sector, as well as being subject to various agricultural colonization schemes. It was not until the later 1920s and 1930s that the "gold belt" of Quebec came into production, marked by the founding of the town of Val d'Or in 1934. Near that community the Sisco mine, which began operations in 1930, produced $40 million worth of gold over the next nineteen years; Beattie Gold mines produced $28 million in the same period. (In comparison, the Hollinger mines at Timmins extracted $169.2 million in gold between 1910 and 1931.) Another large producer of gold in Quebec was the mine at Noranda, which began operations in 1927. Although primarily a copper mine, Noranda concentrated on gold and silver after the bottom fell out of the copper market in the 1930s.

One of the best things about the gold mines of northern Ontario and Quebec was that they prospered during the Great

Depression of the 1930s, especially when the American government raised the fixed price of gold from $20 to $35 per ounce. When Canada devalued its dollar at the outbreak of World War II, the price rose to $38.50. The Sudbury mining region also prospered, mostly because International Nickel Company was such a large producer of nickel that it could control the world price, so that although production fell early in the 1930s before rising again, the price remained almost unchanged between 1929 and 1939. The gold mines also had a marked multiplier effect on the local and provincial economies, since they all needed an elaborate infrastructure, including electric generating plants and connections to a railway. The Noranda mine, for instance, depended on a forty-four-mile branch line to the C.N.R. and a new hydro-electric plant on the upper Ottawa River. All this led to the development of new communities across the Provincial Norths. In this respect, at least, the regions proved to be some of the few bright spots in a very gloomy decade.

The railways were the first and for many decades the only modern method of transportation linking the Provincial Norths to the rest of the country. The Canadian Pacific Railway and the transcontinental railways which eventually were merged into the Canadian National Railway linked northern Ontario and Quebec to the south by 1914. Other lines were built specifically to penetrate the Provincial Norths, notably the Northern Ontario Railway, built to Cochrane between 1902 and 1908 and extended to Moosonee after World War I, which actually earned a profit from hauling mining freight in the midst of the depression. Another was the Hudson Bay Railway to Churchill, the transportation Holy Grail of Prairie farmers and the alternative to the hated C.P.R., begun in 1909 and opened in 1929. This route to European markets seemed certain of success, since the port is 1,600 km closer to Europe by sea than is Montreal. But Churchill was a disappointment as an alternative outlet for western grain, mostly because it had only a three-month shipping season, and insurers charged a premium on ships which braved the Hudson Straits. The railway itself, however, became more important when minerals were discovered at Flin Flon and Thompson. A third was British Columbia's great dream of northern empire — the

Pacific Great Eastern (begun in 1912, but not completed to Prince George until 1956 and extended to Fort Nelson in 1971; now the British Columbia Railway). The Great Slave Railway into the Northwest Territories was a post–World War II project (completed in 1965), as were virtually all the highways into the region.

In the Prairie provinces, the standard problems of locating the resources, finding markets, developing transportation systems, and securing workers were complicated by a nuance of Canada's constitutional system. When Manitoba, Alberta and Saskatchewan joined Confederation, the federal government denied the new provinces control over their natural resources. The logic was simple: the government planned to use these resources, particularly agricultural land, to attract settlers and pay the costs incurred by the nation for the development of railways. Giving the provinces control of such valuable resources at a time so fundamentally important to the process of nation-building was deemed risky and inappropriate. Ottawa held on to control of these resources for more than half a century, not finally surrendering control of them until 1930.

There were in any case fewer dreams of northern empire in Manitoba and Saskatchewan than elsewhere in Canada before World War II, as well as less money to make them realities. The energies of the provincial governments were occupied for the most part with settling the agricultural lands, and when that pioneering task was done, with coping with the catastrophe of depression and drought which followed close on its heels. John Bracken's Progressive government in Manitoba, for instance, declined in 1928 to become involved in a publicly owned hydro project in northwestern Ontario on the grounds of expense. What mining, hydro, and forestry development took place in those two Provincial Norths before 1940 — and there was considerable activity, particularly in the mining sector — was largely carried out by private interests.

Control of these resources was vital to provincial growth and development. It gave the government which held it the authority to dispose of land, regulate the use of rivers and lakes, set and collect royalties on minerals and timber, and otherwise control and regulate the development of the resource sector. Because the direct financial benefits from resource development in the Prairie provinces went to the federal government, their governments were decidedly less enthusiastic than those of the older provinces about supporting mineral and other resource developments in their provinces. Ironically, the gift of control over this sector of their economies came in 1930, the first full year of the depression.

While the depression generally dampened the prospects for mineral development, particularly in isolated, northern districts, there was a surprisingly golden glint to the entire era, caused by the buoyant prices of precious metals throughout the 1930s. In that period of economic turmoil, promoters, honest and crooked, exploited the public's seemingly insatiable interest in gold properties. Stock exchanges and "bucket shops" in Canada and the United States floated shares, some for bona fide properties, others — the infamous "penny dreadfuls" — for bogus holdings. Some purchases bought little more than hope, a fleeting promise of no more value than a lottery ticket; others bought part of a hole in the ground, seemingly solid evidence of the promoters' good intention, but more often a sign of the investors' gullibility. The golden preoccupation continued throughout the depression years, marked by a continual stream of announcements about promising new properties in Ontario, Quebec, Manitoba and British Columbia.

Since northern Manitoba was fortunate to possess a large portion of the Canadian Shield, it too was able to participate in the mining boom of the post–World War I era. The first important activity centred on the curiously-named town of Flin Flon, where a prospector found deposits of copper and zinc in 1914–1915. But the wealth did not fall easily into the hands of investors and miners, for mining the base metals from hard rock required technology far more sophisticated and expensive than the placer gold mining of the Yukon, which even at its most elaborate — hydraulic mining and dredging — was just really panning and sluicing on a larger scale. At Flin Flon it took fourteen years and $25 million in 1920s dollars to bring Hudson Bay Mining and Smelting into production: shafts had to be dug to prove the size of the reserve, a process involving flotation had to be developed to process the crushed ore, a hydro-electric plant built at Island Falls, Saskatchewan, a concentrating plant, copper smelter, zinc plant, and rail line to the Hudson Bay railway built. Then the depression almost put the company out of business when the price of copper fell; only tiny amounts of silver and gold in the ore — less than 0.9 ounce, or about $30 of gold per ton of ore — kept it going. Another company, Sherritt-Gordon, opened a copper-zinc mine in 1931 north of Flin Flon, but it lacked gold deposits and had to close.

Not all areas of the Provincial Norths saw major mineral developments in this period. Just before the turn of the century, northern Alberta had enjoyed some transitory benefits from the Klondike gold rush. Edmonton, revealing the self-interest and greed that often characterizes urban boosterism, touted itself as a logical, all-Canadian route to the Klondike, even though the route was an impractical nightmare which killed a number of those gullible enough to try it. As the prospectors pushed northward, constructing improvements to the transportation facilities along the route from Edmonton to the Mackenzie River and an even worse trail to Fort St. John and northwest to the Yukon, they left a minor but important legacy for the area.

There was one rich resource in northern Alberta that was easily identified but that for years remained undeveloped — the Athabasca tar sands. Early fur traders had described them, but as the Canadian oil industry developed in the early twentieth century, scientists and developers were unsure of how to deal with this unusual resource. Considerable scientific and engineering thought was devoted to the problem of turning the oily glop of the tar sands into a usable product, but with no great success. The mere existence of the tar sands fueled enthusiastic forecasts about the economic future of northern Alberta, an optimistic outlook that only strengthened with the discovery of oil at Norman Wells, Northwest Territories in 1920. For now, however, the resource had to be left in the ground — a tantalizing and frustrating reminder of what the North might be.

Northern Saskatchewan and Labrador, as the post-war era would demonstrate, held considerable mineral potential, but the exploitation of their resources would have to wait. The extreme isolation of these areas, and absence of any suitable transportation system, limited the prospects of any significant mining activity. These two areas, in fact, scarcely made a dent on the general consciousness and generated little of the excitement and optimism that accompanied southern assumptions about other regions of the Provincial Norths.

While mining conformed closely to southern assumptions about the Provincial Norths, considerable attention was devoted to agricultural development, a much less "northern" activity. The settlement of the Canadian west was, it should be remembered, something of an act of faith that defies much conventional wisdom about the possibility of developing commercial agriculture north of the forty-ninth parallel. The entire Canadian prairie was, after all, dismissed for much of the nineteenth century as frozen wasteland too dry to farm. Scientific explorations by Hind and Palliser challenged these assumptions, which were not entirely wrong, and led to the settlement of the prairies after 1870. But there was no consensus on just where the northern limit of commercial agriculture should be drawn. Regional climatic patterns ensured that, once again, latitude was of little use. Rich fingers of farm land extended further north than many had originally expected; the valuable Swan River Valley in Manitoba and the area around Prince Albert, Saskatchewan attracted hundreds of settlers. By the end of the first decade of the twentieth century, the areas of obvious and easy agricultural settlement in the West, as in the East, had been exploited. The St. Lawrence River valley and contiguous regions had been settled many decades before, as had the rich farm lands of southern Ontario. Now the vast western plains were substantially full, as were the much smaller patches of agricultural lands in British Columbia.

The mystique of the social value of agricultural settlement persisted in Canada, however, as did the belief that rich pockets of cultivatable soil remained to be exploited. This belief was particularly strong in Quebec, where it combined with nationalistic and cultural forces to produce a unique movement to "colonize" the northern frontier of the province, a movement which was supported not only by the usual business and political interests, but by the Roman Catholic church as well. The impetus to set up agricultural colonies, which began in earnest in the 1880s, was seen as a means of stopping the serious loss of young people to the United States, where they and their children would eventually become assimilated, losing their language and faith. Northern Quebec thus became at the end of the nineteenth century a powerful symbol of the survival and growth of the francophone population and culture in North America.

Unlike northern Ontario, where prospective settlers were dealt with individually, the government of Quebec recruited its colonists in groups, typically as "colonization societies," which were as often as not headed or strongly influenced by the clergy. Some colonies clustered around religious institutions, such as in the Dolbeau district north of Lake St. John, where a colony grew in the wake of a Trappist monastery founded on the Mistassini River in 1891. The most famous colonization agent was a priest, Father F. X. A. Labelle, who was reputed to have founded sixty settlements in northern Quebec, especially in the county that bears his name. Again, unlike almost every other part of the Provincial Norths to be settled in the post-Confederation period, northern Quebec was settled by people who were racially and culturally homogeneous; even morally so, for in some cases the parish priest had to attest to the good character of would-be colonists.

But faith and good character were not always enough to overcome poor land, and when the colonies were established on marginal soil they tended not to flourish, even though the clergy maintained that in keeping with "les moeurs, les idées, les besoins religieux et moraux des Canadiens-Français," the profit motive was secondary in importance to following a pious life. In some cases the colonists cut down and sold off the timber, then departed; other places grew into permanent communities. It was overall one of the most remarkable manifestations of the nineteenth century Roman Catholic view of what Quebec society should be. The best-known expression of its *zeitgeist* is Louis Hémon's novel *Maria Chapdelaine*, published in 1914, for decades a staple of anglophone high-school French literature courses.

Nor was this entirely a nineteenth century movement. After slowing in the early years of this century, it found new life during the depression of the 1930s. Between 1931 and 1941, 145 new settlements were founded, the majority in the Témiscamingue and Abitibi regions; the population of the former doubled in that period and the latter almost tripled.

The government of Ontario, lacking the same social and nationalistic goals as its Quebec counterpart, did not put the same emphasis on agricultural settlement. As its Provincial North was surveyed, the lands were classified according to whether they were suitable for agriculture or not. Townships designed for homesteading were opened up in the Lake Timiskaming district, around Sault Ste. Marie, on Manitoulin and St. Joseph islands, and west of Lake Superior before the end of the nineteenth century. In some places the land was for sale, in others it was granted for free if the settler would live on it and improve it. The province provided support by way of roads, school grants, police and other government services. Settlers were on their own as individuals to choose (with the help of pamphlets and guidebooks) whatever land they thought best and to make the best of it they could, in marked contrast to the Quebec system. The depression saw the end of official attempts to colonize the pockets of farm land in the province's North; the Hepburn government, elected in 1934, cancelled them as a waste of money. Overall, attempts in the province to settle pioneers in the clay belt and elsewhere had not been very successful; one study showed that 72 percent of the agricultural land settled in northern Ontario between 1912 and 1937 had been abandoned.

The extension of agricultural settlement into northern British Columbia also lacked the nationalist overtones of the French Canadians' move onto the thin soils of the Canadian Shield. In the case of the western province, the rich lands of the Peace River district were an attractive lure, even without an extensive road and railway network in the area. Although the first settlers moved into the area in the early twentieth century, activity picked up after World War I, as returned soldiers capitalized on government land grants offered by the Soldier Settlement Board; a substantial trickle of settlers into the region led to the expansion of new agricultural settlements at Dawson Creek and Fort St. John and, a short distance across the border, at Grande Prairie, Alberta. The Peace River had agricultural potential, but was distant from markets and supply centres. Although much of it was part of British Columbia, the region was in reality tributary to Alberta, particularly Edmonton. Its wheat went to market via Dawson Creek and then Edmonton, since before World War II it had no direct rail or road access to southern British Columbia.

The Peace River country enjoyed a second boom during the depression years. As the dusty grip of the dry years took their toll on Prairie farmers, particularly in south-eastern Alberta and southern Saskatchewan, a number of farmers hitched up their Bennett buggies (cars with their engines removed, hitched to a horse — derisively named after the depression prime minister) and headed north to the Peace River country. Geography had blessed this region with more favourable rainfalls, and the lateness of agricultural settlement in the area ensured that the follies of capitalist agriculture and the abuse of the soil that characterized intensive plains agriculture in this era had not yet been visited upon the region. At a time when much of the West saw a permanent outmigration of rural population, the Peace River country experienced a steady increase in its population. But this was not an influx of rich migrants and developers, for most of the new settlers came with little beyond their experience and knowledge, rudimentary tools and the eternal optimism of the Prairie farmers.

Northern farmers from Quebec to British Columbia were defying assumptions and expectations more than geography. The land was more or less suitable — better in some places than others — the climate supported commercial grains or at least hay for cattle, and if transportation systems were not immediately in place, governments generally responded to regional protests and began construction of the railways, local roads and other facilities deemed essential to settlement in the region. These northward migrations, with the important exception of the French Canadian movement into the Canadian Shield, attracted little outside attention; the country had seemingly used up its enthusiasm for agricultural settlement with the end of the prairie boom shortly before World War I. The expansion of agriculture into the Provincial Norths remained shrouded in anonymity, placing an additional burden on settlers attempting to push back the frontiers of commercial agriculture.

Along with the expansion of agriculture into the Provincial Norths came the development of the region's forest reserves. Timber is, with fur and fish, part of the great troika which supported the early Canadian economy. Of the three, it is the one which is most viable today, and (except in British Columbia, where it operates province-wide, especially in the coastal areas) is also now the one most clearly identified with the Provincial Norths. The harvestable timber of southern Ontario and Quebec was mostly gone by Confederation, but in the Provincial Norths there were seemingly limitless stands of marketable trees. While the early nineteenth century timber trade had been based on the cutting of the hardwood trees of southern Canada for use in shipbuilding and construction, the forest industry of the Provincial Norths, while still producing large quantities of lumber, was also based on the cutting of spruce for the manufacture of pulp and paper. As with mining, exploitation of this resource depended on the extension of railroads and the development of hydro-electric power and new technologies. Where spruce trees, substantial rivers, and railroads were found in the same area, the pulp industry flourished, though not all the mills were in the North; there was, for instance, a large mill at Thorold, Ontario (in the Niagara region), which used logs brought from considerable distances. Much of the early development occurred in northern Quebec, at Chicoutimi, Shawinigan Falls, on the St. Maurice River, and at a number of other locations. There was also development on a smaller scale in the northern forests of the Prairie provinces near towns like The Pas. In Quebec, the forest industry, which employed thousands of people in the mills and cutting logs in the forest, was hailed with joy by nationalists and the clergy, who saw it, like agricultural colonization, as an alternative to emigration and deracination. By 1911 there were twenty-five pulp and twenty paper mills operating in the province, which was the largest producer in Canada, surpassing Ontario by about a third. In Ontario, the industry led to the growth of communities like Dryden and Thunder Bay (until 1970 Port Arthur and Fort William).

Pulp and paper mills required large capital investments, and the companies, often controlled by American interests, wanted assurances that a stable and long-term source of raw materials would be available, preferably by means of long leases over large areas at low prices. By 1929 over 80,000 square miles of Quebec had been granted or leased to the forest and hydro industry; the figure in Ontario for 1940 was over 92,000 square miles. Though the provinces received considerable sums for these leases, they also incurred large expenses in administration, particularly in protecting the trees through forest management and fire prevention and fighting — Ontario spent half its forest revenue in this way in the 1920s. There was also much controversy over the amount of money that flowed to provincial treasuries, and provincial governments were more than once accused of selling timber berths to their friends at artificially low prices. Nevertheless, despite protests, the forest industry was very lightly regulated before World War II.

Production of hydro-electricity was, as previously mentioned, a logical outgrowth of both the mining and the forest industry. It also seemed a natural for the Provincial Norths, with their large rivers and spaces for reservoirs which were unoccupied by anyone except the Native people, who would presumably not object if they were summarily shifted from one place to another in the name of industrial progress. By 1900 it seemed as though a new dam was being built every year somewhere in northern Quebec and Ontario to supply the industries and the growing communities which surrounded them. Whereas most of the power produced in Quebec came from privately owned companies (Shawinigan Water and Power is perhaps the best known) and was sold to industry or exported, in Ontario the publicly owned Ontario Hydro Corporation moved into the northern regions of the province in the 1920s, and by the 1930s power was coming from northern Ontario over the corporation's high voltage lines to Toronto. At the outbreak of World War II it was operating seventy-four generating stations, producing three times as much power as its private competitors, and was importing power from Quebec. Only a few hydro-electric sites were developed in the Provincial Norths west of Ontario before the war, notably at Island Falls in Saskatchewan, and in a few locations in British Columbia, and at Seven Sisters and Slave Falls in the Shield country of Manitoba.

Despite all this development activity, the region maintained a low political profile. But given the small scale of non-Native settlement, this is not surprising. The northward extension of provincial boundaries in the decades after 1870 gave southern politicians control over vast internal colonies, lands and resources which could be used for the future benefit of urban and southern residents. The fundamental assumption underlying plans for northern development was that such initiatives had to have wider goals than bringing jobs and other benefits to regional residents; in most cases, in fact, northern development could occur only if migrants were attracted into the area to work on the construction sites or in the mining or timber camps. Until the post–World War II era, provincial politicians, with the exceptions already mentioned, paid little attention to their northern areas. The reasons for this were simple: politicians were amply occupied with southern problems and possibilities, and the provincial governments lacked the financial and, in the Prairie provinces, the constitutional resources necessary to encourage resource exploitation. Equally important, but often overlooked, is the fact that the Provincial Norths produced almost no prominent politicians of their own. For much of the pre–World War II period, the provincial political system provided few opportunities for representatives from the northern periphery and they, in turn, were generally unable to bring northern concerns to the forefront of the provincial political agenda.

In British Columbia, provincial politics generally divided along traditional lines, with representatives from Vancouver Island, Vancouver and the southern interior vying for control of the political landscape. There were a few attempts to place northern concerns on the agenda, typically in the form of subsidized railway schemes, but the efforts enjoyed slight success. Simon Fraser Tolmie, Conservative premier in the late 1920s, tried to interest the province in a grand scheme to develop a major road to the North, but the plan foundered. Duff Pattullo's abortive attempt to extend the province's northern boundary to the Beaufort Sea has already been described.

The northern regions of the provinces did even less well on the national stage. In the period from Confederation to World War II, when such well-defined and self-conscious regions as the Maritimes, the Prairie West and British Columbia struggled for a place on the national stage, it is hardly surprising that the Provincial Norths were unable to carve out a clear and well-defined place on the political scene. Northern regions were nominally incorporated as northern adjuncts of more populous southern and urban-based constituencies until their populations grew; representatives had difficulty in visiting the outlying districts and incorporating their aspirations into national political platforms. Even today, the federal constituencies which include areas in the Provincial Norths such as Churchill in northern Manitoba or the Patricia district of northern Ontario are enormous, making it very difficult for their members of Parliament to deal with their concerns, despite the advantages of modern communications. Furthermore there was scarcely a hint that the political representatives of the northern provincial zones had a sense of common cause; MPs pushed British Columbian or Quebec causes, fought the political battles of Saskatchewan or Ontario, and rarely came together in any form of common cause which might indicate the embryonic beginnings of a regional identity.

Without a cadre of regional representatives to address the specific needs and interests of the Provincial Norths, the federal government, not surprisingly, paid little attention to the area. The government had little time for northern concerns generally — the Territorial North enjoyed no better success in attracting federal attention — and devoted the country's limited political and financial capital to the substantial and pressing concerns of railway construction, regional protest, urban working class unrest, agricultural settlement and industrial expansion. There was, as yet, no national agenda for the incorporation and development of the vast Middle North, and would not be until the 1950s.

It would be inappropriate and misleading to suggest that the federal and provincial politicians' sorry ignorance of and indifference to the Provincial Norths flew in the face of a coherent and vocal articulation of regional demands. But in all of the provinces, the populations of the northern regions rarely put together a sustained critique of either federal or provincial policies (or the lack thereof); there were occasional protests over specific policies, particularly related to railway development, but no regionally-based northern political visions, either at the provincial or national level.

Why did the non-Native settlers not, in the fashion of Prairie farmers or coastal settlers in British Columbia, quickly develop a regional response to this lack of political attention? There is a simple explanation — many of the non-Native inhabitants were temporary residents. Most of the mining, logging, and construction camps attracted a temporary, mobile workforce. Transient, mostly male workers, typically lacking the full set of social institutions, demonstrated little commitment to the region. They had come, in the well-established pattern of northern workers, to make as much money as they could, as quickly as possible. Whether construction workers or loggers, only a small percentage had any intention of settling permanently in the area. This was not a solid foundation for the development of a regional society. The exceptions were those who worked in the enterprises which survived over the decades in communities like Kirkland Lake, Noranda, and Timmins. The workers in other places were often mobile, remaining in the region while work or inclination lasted; only a tiny percentage of the workers attracted into the region to work on the railways, roads or other temporary construction projects remained in the Provincial Norths when the projects were finished. Many of the loggers were seasonal workers, operating farms in the south and raising money to support their agriculture activities by working in the timber camps; others farmed in the North and moved from one place to another within the region. Some miners moved about routinely, following the new discoveries and the promising camps. There was a considerable rate of attrition and turnover even among the agricultural settlers. In the absence of modern, well-planned company towns with plenty of amenities — the postwar towns like Thompson, Elliot Lake, and Tumbler Ridge — few miners had the opportunity to bring their families with them into the North. Native people, the dominant group of permanent residents in the Provincial Norths, did not participate in provincial or federal politics, and hence lacked the political voice or experience necessary to press an alternative view of northern policies advanced by the largely transient non-Native population and the dominant southern electorate.

By the end of the 1930s, the northern regions had experienced the initial stages of integration into their larger provincial units, but remained very much on the periphery. Portions of the infrastructure were in place, particularly as a result of railway construction in Manitoba and Ontario, but the promise of the early twentieth century had only been partially realized. Mineral development in northern Ontario, Quebec and Manitoba provided substantial proof of the richness of the Canadian Shield, but the resources were hard won and did not sustain the massive booms that the promoters' dreams had envisioned. Perhaps surprisingly, the next substantial impetus for change came from outside the region, and even outside the country.

The onset of war, and particularly the Americans' entry into the war in December 1942, added questions of national security, Allied war effort and defence preparedness to the regional equation. World War II represented a major turning point in the history of the Territorial North. Within weeks after the attack on Pearl Harbor, the United States received permission from Ottawa to build a highway from Dawson Creek across northern British Columbia and the Yukon to Alaska. The stated purpose of the road was to provide a communications and transportation link between the lower forty-eight states and Alaska that was not susceptible to Japanese attack. The construction of Northwest Defence Projects — the Alaska Highway, CANOL project, Northwest Staging Route, Haines Highway and ancillary projects — brought sweeping changes to the Yukon Territory and Mackenzie River valley. In the East, the air bases constructed in conjunction with Project Crimson transformed the economic and social foundations of important areas in the Eastern Arctic. While the significance of these largely American initiatives to the Territorial North is generally understood, far less attention has been paid to the transformative impact of World War II on the Provincial Norths.

The Alaska Highway and the CANOL project, to start with the most well-known of the war-time undertakings, were developed with a view toward the defence of Alaska, but had great significance for northern Alberta and British Columbia. The initial planning for the defence projects centred on Edmonton, Alberta, and a substantial portion of the personnel and supplies for the Canadian sections of the projects passed through the Alberta capital. "Mile Zero" of the Alaska Highway was in Dawson Creek, British Columbia, the northwest terminus of the Canadian rail system at that time; construction work associated with this pivotal construction project — the pioneer road was completed in 1942 in less than eight months — resulted in a vastly improved road from Dawson Creek to Fort St. John and points north. Dawson Creek, Fort St. John and the old trading post at Fort Nelson expanded rapidly and became major beneficiaries of American-financed construction activity. The CANOL project was designed to carry oil from Norman Wells, Northwest Territories to Whitehorse, Yukon, and most of the effort focused on that area. But in order to get supplies and workers to the area, major improvements to the warehousing and transportation facilities in northern Alberta were required.

While the period of intense construction activity in the northwest lasted less than two years, its impact was extensive and permanent. In addition to the Alaska Highway, military planners constructed a string of airfields from Edmonton, Alberta to Fairbanks, Alaska. Support facilities, including a regional telephone network, local roads, improved sewer and water lines in the towns, recreational facilities and the like, were constructed throughout the region. The passage of thousands of workers, soldiers and civilians, Americans and Canadians, through the district brought social disruption and occasional conflict to the once-isolated towns; but the construction workers and soldiers also brought new business opportunities. Northern British Columbia and northern Alberta had been truly transformed by the friendly and short-term American military "invasion." The new facilities, and particularly the transportation infrastructure that accompanied the military projects, provided the regional tools necessary to deal with the economic and social changes of the post-war era.

While the effects of military operations were less pronounced in more eastern districts, wartime construction nonetheless brought important changes. Project Crimson, for example, built to allow for the ferrying of airplanes to England, required a series of support airfields through northern Manitoba. The bases at The Pas and Churchill, in particular, provided both short-term construction jobs for people in the area and left a legacy for the post-war era in the form of modern air fields and supporting facilities. Churchill in particular was a beneficiary of the cold war, and prospered in the 1950s as a rocket launching site and research centre. Its population in 1960 was about 6,000, but it has declined in the past thirty years to 1,100, and the town survives precariously as a grain shipment port, and increasingly as a destination for tourists who come to see its famous polar bears and beluga whales. Northern Ontario became home base for a variety of military projects — primarily under control of the Canadian government and not, like the Northwest Defence Projects and Project Crimson, American-dominated activities. A series of air corps training centres were built in the northern reaches of the province, as were several internment camps for prisoners of war and other "enemies of the state" — including a number of German-Canadian and Italian-Canadian internees and conscientious objectors.

Newfoundland, then not a part of Canada, played a vital role in the Allied war effort. A large American military presence, particularly by the air force, occupied the former dominion, which had effectively gone bankrupt and reverted to colonial status during the depression. The Canadian government, already casting covetous eyes toward Newfoundland, took an active interest in American activities in the area. A massive, American-built airforce complex at Goose Bay, Labrador, was the cornerstone of Allied operations in the northern zone. Military activities did not extend significantly beyond Goose Bay, although post-war research revealed, somewhat distressingly, that the Germans had established weather and communications sites at remote sites in the region.

As historian Shelagh Grant has described, World War II ushered in a strikingly new era in the history of the Canadian North. Wartime activities, particularly the Canadian government's gift to the Americans of a virtual free hand in the construction of military facilities, alerted the country to the possibility that its claims to northern sovereignty might be at risk. The establishment of the office of Special Commissioner for Northwest Defence Projects, and the appointment of Brigadier-General W. W. Foster to the position in 1943, revealed the first glimmers of a new attitude regarding national obligations towards the Canadian North.

The Territorial North — still under federal government control — became the primary beneficiary of the new approach to the Canadian North. But the Provincial Norths had been significantly recast by the wartime activities, especially the American-directed construction initiatives. Many of the facilities were closed down, abandoned or dismantled in the immediate post-war era. But the downsizing did not eliminate the new roads, airfields and improved municipal facilities — Dawson Creek and Fort St. John never shrank to their pre-war size, for example — nor could such actions strip away the new sense of connectedness and integration that accompanied the arrival of hundreds if not thousands of southern workers and soldiers into isolated corners of the Provincial Norths.

World War II had, in a profound and permanent way, placed the Provincial Norths on the maps and in the minds of policy makers across Canada and even in portions of the United States. With modern airfields, new roads, the improvement of river facilities, massive amounts of vacant warehouse space, and the other logistical detritus of military occupation, the Provincial Norths now had something more tangible to offer would-be settlers and developers. Of course there were still massive gaps, particularly in Saskatchewan, northern Ontario and northern Quebec, which still remained far outside the network of transportation and support facilities.

But perhaps the most important change from the wartime era is also the least tangible. Before the war, the Provincial Norths had been easy to ignore. Only rich and relatively accessible resources attracted attention; southerners were rarely convinced that rhetoric of expansion and growth held much real promise. The war had, however, pushed back the "frontier" considerably, opening southern eyes to the prospects for future development in the region. It was easy, to use northern British Columbia as an example, to dismiss a region with no road and only rudimentary air access; now, thanks to American military construction, the region boasted a reasonably good road and promising air facilities, and was clearly an integral part of the province.

Canadians, retaining the slow, plodding and southern-oriented outlook that had so long characterized this nation that has been seemingly anchored to the U.S. border, moved slowly to capitalize on the possibilities raised by the wartime projects. But the groundwork had been laid, improvements to infrastructure were, at least in some areas, in place. Perhaps most important, the federal government and its provincial counterparts were more predisposed to look favourably on this long-ignored part of the country. The post-war period would see striking changes in the southern approach to the Provincial Norths and, consequently, a massive shift in patterns of development and settlement. No group was to be more affected by these changes than the region's indigenous inhabitants.

Chapter Four

The Original Inhabitants

Most Canadians living in the southern regions of the country see the North in three ways: as a place of "adventure," either actual or vicarious, as a source of romantic inspiration — especially for central Canadians — and as a source of potential riches. The aboriginal peoples, on the other hand, have always viewed the North simply as a homeland, the land of their ancestors' birth and of their own, a land where they expect to spend their lives, and where they hope to see their children grow and prosper. The typical pattern of non-Native involvement with the region, particularly before the twentieth century, has been to move north, develop and exploit the available resources — furs, minerals — and then leave. The indigenous inhabitants have been compelled to invent strategies to react and adapt to these invasions of newcomers.

The period between Confederation in 1867 and the end of the Second World War as it applies to the First Nations of the Provincial Norths is a history of these adaptations. The essential point of this transformation is, however, that it was one of degree rather than kind. This point needs to be stressed, and explained, since it would seem at first glance that the lives of these people must have changed tremendously between 1867 and 1945. This was the era that saw the arrival of modern technology in the Provincial Norths: the outboard motors, the wireless radios, the bush planes — all of which must surely have had a dramatic effect on their lives. Yet outboard motors, for example, like the firearms which the indigenous people had acquired in an earlier generation, were simply devices that enhanced the efficiency of what they were already doing: hunting, fishing, gathering, and trapping. Just as a novelist is no less a writer because she uses a word processor rather than a steel-nibbed pen, so a Cree hunter is no less a hunter because he uses an outboard motor on his canoe rather than paddling it, or has his supplies flown in to a remote lake by a bush pilot rather than carrying them on his back.

The more important changes which began in this period were social rather than technical — events such as the founding of mission schools in the Provincial Norths and the efforts of missionaries at spiritual and social transformation. And even these changes were controlled or at least influenced to a considerable degree by the First Nations people before World War II. The mission schools, now so vigorously excoriated by Native people as destroyers of their culture, were a much less pernicious influence before the war, simply because there was so much less pressure on people to send their children to them, and they were relatively few in number. Because the Native people could send their children or not, as they chose, the missionaries, who were anxious to extend their influence over them through educating their children, had to conduct themselves so as not to alienate them; a very different situation from that which was to exist a generation later.

To the indigenous people of the Provincial Norths, the achievement of Confederation in 1867 had little immediate impact. While the politicians of the fledgling nation dreamed of continental greatness and a transcontinental railway, aboriginal life in the region continued much as it had at the beginning of the nineteenth century, mostly revolving around the economic dictates of the fur trade. First Nations and non-Native people continued to meet, as they had for centuries, at isolated posts: Fort George and Eastmain in Quebec, Moosonee and Fort Severn in Ontario, Norway House and York Factory in Manitoba, Lac La Ronge and Cumberland House in Saskatchewan, Fort Vermilion in Alberta, Fort Nelson and Dease Lake in British Columbia. The indigenous people continued to move freely about their traditional lands; only in a few places, such as the more southerly parts of the Provincial Norths in Ontario and Quebec, were their paths hindered by railways, logging, or mining operations, or, as in British Columbia in the mid-1920s, by a scheme of trapline registration. The traditional family areas of hunting and trapping were still mostly intact, and the people who had always used them continued to do so in the extended family groups which were part of their culture, visiting the trading posts when they wanted or needed to, and gathering in larger band groups as the seasons permitted, or hunting or other cultural needs dictated.

Superficially, it appeared that the lives of the indigenous people of the Provincial Norths had changed a great deal in this period. Certainly the rapid absorption of manufactured goods, tools, and clothing made it appear at first glance that the values at the core of their lives must have altered as well. Non-Natives who wished the Native people well — they were "assimilationists" in an era when almost everyone thought that assimilation was the best thing for Natives — were inclined to see the adoption of these goods as a sign of the inevitability of cultural change and a healthy adaptation of the superior European way of life. But this was not the way the Native people viewed the process. Though they had adopted the artifacts of European life, at least insofar as the artifacts served their own purposes, they had not adopted the philosophical foundation which underlay these goods. They had not adopted, for instance, the idea of the accumulation of private capital, nor the abandonment of social and cultural responsibilities in favour of the maximization of profits. Just because a Native person wore European clothes, cooked in an iron pot, and hunted with a rifle did not mean that he had accepted a European value system.

In some ways, however, the First Nations people of the Provincial Norths in the decades after Confederation had lost more of their traditional culture than they realized at the time. While they continued to hunt and trap, they no longer did so to secure animals for their own use, but according to the dictates of the fur trade, which was changing dramatically throughout the nineteenth century. The most notable change was that the beaver, the prime pelt since the beginning of the trade in Canada, had been displaced after mid-century by the shift in European fashion from felt hats to ones made of silk or other fabric. Instead, different furs, particularly luxury furs like silver fox, marten, and mink, became highly prized. The Hudson's Bay Company, the generations-old rock upon which the entire industry was based, underwent a radical change after Confederation. As the nineteenth century waned it became less a northern fur company and more a real estate company interested in maximizing the returns from its prairie lands. By 1900 it was evident that the Company's future lay in commercial retailing; the process which finally led to the recent sale of all its northern posts and the total abandonment of its fur-trading business could have been predicted even then. This process held an advantage for the Native people: rival companies, some large, others consisting of a single trader, moved into the trade, stimulating competition which resulted in the improvement of the trappers' returns. In northern Ontario, for instance, there were thirty independent traders working north of the Canadian National Railway line, especially around Cochrane, who sold to Montreal dealers, and provided vigorous competition for the HBC. The same was true of the other Provincial Norths.

Though some historians have suggested that the fur trade was dying after 1870, this was clearly not the case, and recent research has shown that it continued after that year much as before, though subject to continuous change. When fashions altered, so did the fur markets and thus the economy of the Provincial Norths. At one time the price of silver fox sky-rocketed, leading to unprecedented prosperity in regions where the animals could be trapped. At other times, unpredictably, the price dropped, leading to some hardship. This boom and bust pattern continued until a catastrophic collapse in the late 1940s from which the industry never really recovered. But in the period between Confederation and World War II the fur trade remained the economic foundation of aboriginal life, though often a declining one, providing the material goods and necessities of life in the region.

The First Nations people neither knew nor cared what was going on in the corporate boardrooms of firms like the Hudson's Bay Company, much as decisions made there would have a marked effect on their prosperity. Their concerns were more practical: was there a trading post nearby (or better still, two of them, to stimulate some competition); were fur prices high enough to permit them to clear their debts at the post and purchase the goods needed to operate another year; were there enough animals on the land for a good harvest and to perpetuate the species for another year?

Though the basic underpinning of life remained the same for the indigenous people, the new technology of the twentieth century certainly changed the appearance of their lives, and made them more efficient hunters. The outboard motor expanded the area which one man could trap and made it far easier to travel up-river and safer to cross large lakes. New steel traps also improved trapping returns, particularly the leg-hold traps, so detested by modern urban-based animal rights activists. The bush plane provided a means of quick access to isolated settlements and camps, ensuring a steady flow of supplies to the remotest regions, and eventually making it possible to remove the seriously ill to hospitals in urban centres. The outboard motor, the airplane, and the radio, which began to link the Provincial Norths with southern Canada in the 1920s and 1930s, formed the great technological troika which altered the lives, first of the non-Natives of the region (who were in the best position to make use of them), and finally all its inhabitants.

Although there were some years in the twentieth century when the fur trade provided very handsome returns for the Native people, the general trend throughout the century in the Provincial Norths was one of decline. There were many reasons for this, but the basic one was excessive pressure on the stock of fur-bearing animals. The populations of the First Nations, which had been devastated in the nineteenth century and earlier by disease, began to rebound in the twentieth, which meant that there were more trappers in a given area. The independent traders who competed with the Hudson's Bay Company also stimulated an increased demand for furs. The result was not only increased production, which eventually led to over-trapping and lower prices, but periodic shortages of food in some areas. The Hudson's Bay Company, still the only economic constant in most parts of the Provincial Norths, responded to these conditions by providing credit to the Native trappers, and, eventually, supplies of food and goods given gratis to those in serious need. The federal government generally compensated it for its benevolence; having the Company's officers act as unpaid welfare agents was a good deal cheaper for the government than shouldering the responsibility itself.

The combination of relief payments and advancement of credit (called "debt" in the trade) permitted the Native people to continue to live and trap in their traditional territories. Viewed from the Company's perspective, the arrangement was advantageous, since it not only permitted the Native people to stay in place, but in a way compelled them to do so. Tied to the Company by bonds of debt, they did not explore other economic alternatives, remaining within the orbit of the fur trade — an arrangement which could in some ways be described as an early version of the welfare system. But as A. J. Ray points out, the old paternalistic relationship between the Native people and the Company was crumbling by 1945, to be supplanted after the war by the welfare state.

Though governments preferred to leave social assistance in private hands (the treaties that were signed in the Provincial Norths in this period had only minimal effect in this direction), the same was not true in the area of regulation of natural resources. As was mentioned in a previous chapter, the provinces in the post-Confederation era moved enthusiastically into the regulation of the forest and mining sectors of their Provincial Norths, and the same was true of wildlife. Before Confederation, what had passed for a northern conservation policy had resulted from the instinctive actions of the indigenous people themselves and the Hudson's Bay Company's desire, based on the same sense of their own interests, to prevent over-hunting and the destruction of resources.

At the beginning of this century, two forces converged in the northern forest: the first was a continent-wide interest in wildlife and conservation; the second was the perceived, and in some cases real, evidence of the over-hunting of fur-bearing animals and other game. The nineteenth century saw many examples of the destruction of species — the extinction of the passenger pigeon and the near-annihilation of the plains bison are the two most notorious. The devastation of huge tracts of forest, particularly in the United States, where tens of thousands of acres were consumed in fires or otherwise wasted, the damage visited upon large areas of states like West Virginia and Pennsylvania, where coal mining and oil drilling made the landscape hideous — these led to a new environmentalism which manifested itself in the establishment of national parks and wildlife refuges, a force which was strengthened by the potential for tourist dollars. The first National Park in the Provincial Norths was Wood Buffalo Park, established across the northern Alberta-Northwest Territories boundary in 1922 to protect the last herd of wood bison. The second, and the only other national park in the Provincial Norths is Pukaskwa, established near Marathon on the Lake Superior shore in 1971, though Prince Albert National Park (1927), which lies partly in Canadian Shield country, might be considered to be in the region as well.

Public concern for the environment (though that word was not used before the war), coupled with the increasing belief that governments had the power and the duty to regulate public use of natural resources, culminated in a series of measures designed to control hunting and trapping. Some of these involved co-operation among governments, such as the international agreements to protect migratory birds, particularly the Migratory Birds Convention Treaty of 1916. Some provinces introduced regulations to control trapping; British Columbia, for instance, in 1926 required all trappers, Native and non-Native, to register for specific areas. In the same period the provinces introduced licensing systems for hunters, and set bag limits for game, birds, and fish, as well as seasonal limits for hunting. The purpose was partly to protect the livelihood and the foodstocks of the indigenous people, but also to protect and regulate a lucrative and rapidly growing part of the tourist industry. At the same time the provinces began to recoup some of the administrative expenses of regulation by imposing a royalty on furs.

In some provinces these regulations were enforced by a provincial police force (Ontario, Quebec, British Columbia until 1950), and in the Prairie provinces (after 1932) by the R.C.M.P., in co-operation with provincial wildlife officers; in Labrador there was no regulation at all before World War II. The new wildlife regulations were in a way the first sign of the heavy hand of government that was to descend on the First Nations people of the Provincial Norths after the war. In reality, though, the regulations did not always have a great effect on them. For one thing, the remote Native communities in the Provincial Norths were not very strictly policed; many had no police presence at all. For another, the legal right of provincial governments to regulate the activities of Native hunters was always uncertain (as to a degree it still is), and the provinces had to tread carefully in this area; attempts to prosecute indigenous people for hunting out of season and similar offences were not always successful.

The fact that Native people continued the age-old activities of hunting and trapping did not mean that they were necessarily resistant to other forms of economic activity. The idea that they opposed wage labour carries a not very subtle suggestion that they were incapable of performing it, or of adjusting to its requirements. Rather, it was that the traditional occupations suited their cultural patterns, of which capitalism and the accumulation of possessions were not a part. Their objection to wage labour was that it ran across the seasonal or periodic patterns of their lives, while trapping could be carried on around these patterns; thus the continuing of the trapping way of life was a matter of choice, not ability. The fact that many First Nations people insisted on returning to the bush periodically to hunt, trap, and fish as the seasons dictated was not only a cultural habit, but was also made necessary by the uncertain nature of the fur trade. If game was scarce, or if prices fell, it could be difficult to survive on the proceeds of the trapline; the seasonal hunt could therefore be a matter of life and death. But to many non-Natives, these patterns seemed to indicate that the Native people were unreliable as workers, people who worked on "Indian time," as the racist phrase described it.

Nevertheless, indigenous people did find work from time to time within the expanding industrial sector of the Provincial Norths. Only a few found employment on the railroads or in large construction projects; here, prejudice against Natives in the workforce was very strong, and Natives were either not hired, or found the conditions of employment uncongenial. The same was often true of the mining camps, though a larger number of indigenous people worked on an individual basis with prospectors, lending them their invaluable knowledge of local areas. It was in the commercial fishing industry, particularly in northern Manitoba, and in lumber camps all across the Provincial Norths, that Native people were most successful at securing employment for wages. Both of these activities were seasonal, which meant that those who worked in them could count on having long periods off to engage in traditional activities. In a few places, notably in the coastal towns of northern British Columbia, substantial numbers of indigenous people worked inside large factories, particularly in salmon canneries. In other places, a few people with entrepreneurial skills became involved in the business end of the fishing or lumber industry. And in guiding hunters and tourists, another seasonal activity, many Native people also found a source of cash income.

The appearance of Native people in these particular occupations illustrates an important point that is too often overlooked in studying their history. The point is that although they were certainly all too often the victims of forces beyond their control, they were also — more often than some apologists would admit — in charge of their own destinies. The fact that Native people continued to hunt and trap, and those who wanted to work for cash typically wound up in the fishing or lumber industry rather than an industrial enterprise or on a railroad, was by no means entirely the result of racism, though there was plenty of that. Seen from a Native perspective, this was a matter of choice, and was quite logical. The fur trade, with all its fluctuations, provided a great deal of security and continuity, certainly far more than working for some fly-by-night mining promoter or a contractor building a dam who would be in the country only for a season or two. Continued participation in the fur trade was not proof of the victimization of First Nations people (though some were indeed victimized by it), but rather of the fact that they were capable of making decisions that were economically logical, as well as culturally, socially, and spiritually appropriate. The fur trade was a nexus of culture and economics that was entirely suited to the indigenous people of the Provincial Norths.

Because it was at the centre of the aboriginal economy for so many decades, it is only natural that most contacts between the indigenous people and non-Natives occurred within the context of the fur trade. Before the mid-nineteenth century, there existed a well-established pattern of fur traders marrying Native or mixed-blood women. After that date, this pattern gave way to a preference on the part of traders for non-Native wives. The old structure lingered, however, and some traders, particularly those of lower rank in the companies, elected to remain permanently in the North and marry Native women. In general, however, the new pattern prevailed: traders came to the Provincial Norths, either single or with a wife and family, but in either case remained outside the family structure of the Native community. The old bonds of marriage and family, which had previously drawn the traders into the centre of aboriginal life, were replaced by more formal lines of communication and contact based on commerce and divided along racial lines; these tended to separate Natives and non-Natives. Nevertheless, among non-Natives it continued to be the traders who had the best knowledge of Native culture, and who were often the most supportive of it.

Other segments of the non-Native workforce had less reason to interact regularly with the indigenous communities. Unlike the fur traders, whose work drew them into regular and mutually beneficial relations with indigenous people, construction and other workers tended to live in self-contained communities and camps, separated by policy and by choice from the Native people in the surrounding regions. And unlike the fur traders, who had a kind of symbiotic relationship with the indigenous people, these workers brought a different ideology and different assumptions, particularly racial ones, into the Provincial Norths. Their jobs were based on the exploitation, not the preservation and harvesting, of the natural environment and its resources. The Native people were as a rule alarmed by the speed and ferocity of the "development" that took place in their land. The activity which scarred the lands on which they had lived for millennia also helped to erect barriers between them and the newcomers, barriers that were strengthened by the outsiders' tendency to look on them as economically backward and racially inferior.

It is striking, but under these circumstances perhaps not surprising, how small a part was played by the Native people on the development frontier of the Provincial Norths. They appear from time to time in government and police reports, often in connection with activities involving alcohol, activities which the government had decreed illegal, creating new categories of crime and thus many new criminals by legislative fiat. The provisions, one might almost say the paranoia, of the Indian Act in matters relating to alcohol did not eradicate its use among Native people, but did help to buttress the barriers between them and non-Natives. What non-Natives enjoyed as a standard means of recreation was forbidden to Natives, and the authorities expended much energy in trying to keep it so. This policy may have saved a few from the clutches of Demon Rum and was in part well-intentioned, but it did much more harm than good: it changed drinking from a recreational or social activity to an illegal and furtive one; it encouraged binge drinking; it compelled Natives who wished to obtain alcohol to acquire it from the lowest class of non-Natives or to make it themselves; it discredited the legal system in the eyes of Native people; and it illustrated a deep official fear that alcohol would bring out a bestial side of indigenous people that some felt lay not far below the surface of their character.

The new and growing industrial order in the Provincial Norths had an increasing tendency to relegate Native people to its social and economic periphery. Provincial governments became increasingly preoccupied with the issues arising from the growth of the mining and forest industries, and from the new urban centres in the region. The Natives seemed increasingly unimportant, representatives of an old and dying order, who were in any case the responsibility of the federal government. But the old order did not disappear; it remained healthy, perhaps surprisingly so, and hunting, fishing and trapping remained as a strong base until after the end of World War II.

What really eroded the strength of this ancient way of life, besides the weakening of the fur trade economy, was not so much the intrusion of the mining and forest industries — for the Native people could simply avoid them if they wished — but an ultimately irresistible force from quite another direction. This was a benevolent force, bent not on harming or exploiting the indigenous people, or even on entering into mutually beneficial agreements with them, but on helping them, changing them, and "improving" them. First came the missionaries, intent on proselytizing and educating the Native people, on rooting out the "savage" and "heathen" part of their nature; much later the government came, bringing the gift of the welfare state.

Missionaries have been in the Provincial Norths for almost as long as Europeans have been in Canada. French priests penetrated Quebec's north in the seventeenth century, and as early as the 1670s founded a mission to the Nipissings on the north shore of Lake Superior. The Moravians arrived in Labrador in 1752, where they not only converted the Inuit to Christianity, but helped them adapt to the arrival of non-Native settlers, without destroying their culture. Next to preaching the gospel, the missionaries' main activity over the centuries was teaching.

The federal government was glad to support mission schools (which in turn subsidized mission activity generally), since it relieved Ottawa, in its own mind, of the responsibility to do anything more for the Native people. By the 1880s the Grey Nuns had founded a school at Fort Chipewyan in northern Alberta, and by the turn of the century other schools were founded across the region. The usual grant was $150 to $300 per year for a day school, and $72 per child per year for a boarding school. There was more to the mission impulse than conversion and education; the churches also founded the first hospitals in northern Canada, another task which government was happy to delegate to them.

Because the majority of indigenous people continued to move about on a seasonal basis, children attended school only sporadically, or in many cases not at all. Large numbers of children were listed on the school rolls, but many fewer — sometimes only a quarter — were in attendance on any given day. This, combined with the language difficulties experienced by missionary teachers who had come to the North only recently, meant that the amount of useful teaching done was often not much, and as the school reports show, the majority of students did not progress beyond the first few grades.

The solution to the problem advanced by the missionaries was the boarding school. Not only would the students be in class regularly for the greater part of the year, but since they would be away from their parents, they would lose, it was hoped, the indigenous values, habits, and customs which were keeping them primitive and backward, preventing them from becoming well-trained, Christian, obedient, and hygienic Canadians. In some cases, where a settled non-Native community was nearby, the boarding school would be built there and run by the government, but its aims and methods would be much the same as in the church-run schools.

The result of the boarding school experience for many of those who attended them, as anyone who has read a newspaper in the past five years will know, fell short of the design. Because the missionary organizations were always short of money, the schools were often physically substandard, and lack of money also hampered efforts to hire competent lay staff, and to provide adequate nutrition and other care for the children. At some schools discipline was harsh, even savage; the stories of children being beaten for speaking their own language are legion. It is difficult to pass judgement on the activities of the missionaries in the Provincial Norths of the Prairie provinces and British Columbia, since these are currently in the midst of a searing and very public re-appraisal. The horrifying revelations of physical and sexual abuse in church-run boarding schools have led some denominations — the United Church and the Anglican church in particular — to offer general apologies to indigenous people. On the other hand, as anguished former missionary-teachers are at pains to point out, for many years they were the only people to champion the Native cause in government and before the public. And as more than a few Native people have themselves testified, a mission school experience could have real benefits. Whatever the schools were like, however, they all tried to perform a "melting pot" function — to eradicate as much as possible the "Indian" nature of the children — to teach them the habits of cleanliness, punctuality, thrift, and the other values prized by southern Canadians. Since for most there was little chance of employment after leaving school, they returned to their families to face the trauma of being neither entirely Native nor entirely non-Native; some described themselves as "apples" — white on the inside, red on the outside.

The ethnocentrism which prevailed in Canada during the boarding-school era is no more evident than in the fact that no one seems to have asked the Native people what they thought was an appropriate education or how they envisioned their future. Some of them refused to send their children to school, while others, believing that even a poor education was a better defense against the pressures of Euro-Canadian society than none at all, delivered their children to the boarding schools. Some flourished there, others escaped, while others were broken in body and spirit.

The post-Confederation era saw new efforts at evangelism in the Provincial Norths, marked by intense rivalries between Roman Catholics and Protestants. In this rivalry the Catholic church had the great advantage of the more authoritarian structure of their church. The Protestants had perennial difficulties in recruiting for northern Canadian missions, which were distinctly less attractive to candidates than China or Africa, the high profile locations where saving souls seemed more rewarding than in the sub-boreal wastes of Canada. Rome had fewer problems in this regard; its representatives went where they were told, and tended to stay in one place for their entire careers.

The missionaries' success at changing or redirecting the Native spiritual impulse is also problematic, since it is so difficult to assess. As a rule the missionaries in the nineteenth and twentieth centuries met with little resistance or hostility when they arrived in the Provincial Norths, and the baptism and conversion statistics which followed thrilled southern clerics and congregations. There was a general formal acceptance of the liturgy and the social conventions — monogamy and so forth — of Christianity. A few Native people became lay readers or clergy. Though this conversion was not cynical — the Native people were not the "rice Christians" of China — it is unclear to what extent Native spirituality was changed by the missionaries' teaching. For many years it was generally thought that the indigenous people had abandoned "paganism," but now that closer attention is being paid to this aspect of their history, and especially now that they are increasingly speaking for themselves, it appears that much of their spiritual world is still essentially intact. Christianity, which seems to the non-Native world to be all-embracing, is in some ways quite limited. It says a great deal about the relations between people, but, particularly as introduced by the missionaries, it says almost nothing about people's relations with the rest of the physical world — animals, for instance — where the roots of Native spirituality lie. Since they were so different, and operated as it were on different wavelengths, the two systems — the environmentally-based spirituality of indigenous people and the God-centred, codified religion of the missionaries — could co-exist without a great deal of friction, particularly when the Native people remained on the land.

The arrival of government, though initially more tentative and less intrusive in the lives of the indigenous people than that of the missionaries, was ultimately to bring about much greater change. In the first years after Confederation, the federal government, which had the responsibility for Native people under the Indian Act, was unsure of how to deal with the indigenous people of the Provincial Norths. Indian policy for southern Canada was simple enough: the Native people should be moved on to reserves set aside for them, where they could be taught to adapt to the mainstream of Canadian society by becoming farmers, leaving their former lands open to agricultural settlement and development. But this policy made no sense in the Provincial Norths, which were generally unsuitable for agriculture. Since there would presumably never be a large influx of settlers into the Provincial Norths, there was no need to move the Native people on to reserves; the best policy, therefore, was to leave them alone to continue in their traditional pursuits. This policy also had the advantage of being the least costly one.

The Department of Indian Affairs did establish a series of Indian Agencies across the Provincial Norths in places like Berens River, Manitoba, Garden River, Ontario, Escoumains, Quebec, Saddle Lake, Alberta, and Hazelton, British Columbia. Each agent had a huge area and a small budget which was spent on emergency relief for bands which happened to encounter short-term difficulties — scarcity of game and the like, or a serious epidemic of disease. Some of the agents were sympathetic to their charges, while others were harsh, highly ethnocentric petty bureaucrats.

The most significant government initiative in the Provincial Norths in this era was the extension into it of the federal treaty process. Formal agreements between the Native people of

Canada and the Crown had begun long before Confederation, of course, even in parts of the Provincial Norths, such as northern and northwestern Ontario, where the Indians were brought under treaty by the Robinson-Huron and Robinson-Superior Treaties in 1850. The post-Confederation era, however, saw the signing of eleven "numbered" treaties, beginning with Treaty 1, signed outside the walls of Lower Fort Garry, north of Winnipeg, in 1871. Again, the intention of the government in launching this process was to clear the Prairie West of aboriginal title so that agricultural settlement could take place. For this reason, except for Treaty 3 in northwestern Ontario, the Provincial Norths were not included, until some use was found for them by outsiders.

The post-Confederation treaties which affect the Provincial Norths are Treaty 8 (1899) which covers northeast British Columbia, northern Alberta, and part of northern Saskatchewan; Treaty 10 (1906), the rest of northern Saskatchewan; the 1908 extension of Treaty 5, northern Manitoba; and Treaty 9 (1905 and 1929), northern Ontario. The subject of treaties is a complex and contentious one. It should be noted, however, that the Native people were not passive victims of the treaty process, nor did the government force treaty on them against their will. The First Nations people of northern Manitoba, to take a case in point, petitioned the government for years to be taken into Treaty 5, which had originally been signed in 1875. They wanted protection for their traplines against the encroachments of non-Native trappers, and they wanted the cash and other treaty benefits which had been given to those who signed the treaties on the southern prairies. The government ignored these demands for years, until developments such as the proposed railway to Hudson Bay through northern Manitoba made it desirable to settle the question of aboriginal title to land in that part of the province. Then the official position abruptly changed, and the treaty was quickly extended to the northern boundary of Manitoba. This development was welcomed by the Native people. The Chief of the York Factory band wrote to the Minister of the Interior:

We have been quietly waiting for years to be taken in as Treaty people, & now that the Hudson Bay Railroad is coming down our way we hope that the Government will take us under their care. Our hunting lands will be ruined by the shriek of the Iron horse & we will be at a loss to know how to feed & clothe our little ones.

This is not for a moment to say that the Treaties were necessarily advantageous to the indigenous people of the Provincial Norths, only that they often welcomed them. It has been argued, however, though this is not a currently popular position, that the Treaties did act as a kind of buffer for the Native people, giving them at least a measure of protection against exploitation.

Before World War II, the changes confronting the Native people of the Provincial Norths were small and localized, compared to what occurred after 1945. Railways had been built through their lands, treaties had been signed, dams and mines built in places, large tracts of timber harvested, but still the fur trade provided a living, and it was possible to live largely apart from non-Native society. There were government agencies in places, and the missionaries were attempting to educate and change the people, but it was possible to avoid them too. The Native people adopted what seemed useful to them, particularly the new technology, and shunned what they did not want. The first half of this century was thus a period of relative calm; the second half was to see a great deal of turmoil and upheaval, much of it in the name of progress, charity, and social engineering.

Chapter Five

Completing the Colonization of the Provincial Norths

Until the end of the Second World War, much of the Provincial Norths, despite decades of mining and forest development in northern Ontario and Quebec, was still a land of the future, a place that most Canadians thought of either as an inaccessible wasteland or as a repository of resource wealth. Across most of the region the fur trade remained the foundation of the aboriginal economy. But the region's time on the national stage was coming, and the next forty years would see a tremendous surge in the development of Canada's Middle North.

The boom in the Provincial Norths was partly due to the fact that much of the region was "discovered" in the 1940s and 1950s, a process which began in the northwest, for example, with the wartime defence projects. These brought tremendous road, airfield, pipeline, and associated infrastructure construction to wide areas of the region, and alerted Canadian leaders to its economic potential. The activities of Americans during the war, particularly in northern British Columbia and Alberta, and to a lesser extent in places like Goose Bay, Labrador, brought out the old Canadian dog-in-the-manger attitude towards the North: traditionally, Canadians had ignored the country's North until outsiders showed interest in it. This had been the case in the Klondike, and in the eastern and western Arctic, and proved true in much of the Provincial Norths as well.

During the war there had been tens of thousands of American military and civilian workers carrying out various duties in Canada (described in Chapter 3), in most cases with virtually no supervision from Canadians, forming a kind of friendly army of occupation. Having arrived in what was virtually a political vacuum to carry out their duties, they tended to treat the region as *terra nullius*, a fact which alarmed those Canadians who were concerned about northern sovereignty. At war's end, therefore, officials in Ottawa considered means to bring the region more firmly under Canadian control, and ways to sell Canadians on the exciting possibilities they believed could be found in the country's sub-Arctic. Escott Reid, a nationalist and northern enthusiast attached to the Department of External Affairs, believed that northern development could give Canadians a sense of purpose in the post-war era:

> After the emotional debauch of the war there is going to be a bad hangover in all the former belligerent countries. In order that peoples' lives will not feel too empty, some peacetime equivalents to the exciting national objectives to the war must be found. The opening of a new frontier in the Canadian North can, I think, become a national objective of some importance to the Canadian People. Even if, from the point of view of securing the highest possible national income, the Canadian North is not worth a large expenditure of national energy and capital, a very large expenditure might nevertheless be justified in an effort to realize an inspiring and somewhat romantic national objective.

Though Reid's hope was not fully realized — Canadians after the war took as a national objective not the opening of the north, but the avid pursuit of materialism and the good life — it is remarkable for the attitude it displays towards the region. Like the American army, Reid saw the North as a blank slate on which Canadians could write what future they wished as if no one of any importance lived there already. In any case, Canada in the 1940s and early 1950s had other tasks at hand — the cold war and the Korean War in particular — and other nation-building exercises in the south, notably the completion of the Trans-Canada highway and the construction of the St. Lawrence Seaway.

But the idea of northern development was in the air, and in the late 1950s the vision found a prophet in the person of John G. Diefenbaker, leader of the Progressive Conservative party, prime minister from 1957 to 1963, and member of Parliament for many years for Prince Albert, a city on the fringe of the Provincial Norths. In his victorious election of 1957, and in his even more triumphant re-election of 1958, Diefenbaker spoke in ringing words of a "northern vision," his blueprint for a new Canada, facing not the United States, a country which he feared and mistrusted, but northwards:

> To assure economic development in all parts of the country the Conservative Party will offer a new National Policy founded on a renewed sense of national purpose. Whereas Sir John MacDonald [*sic*] was concerned with opening the West, we shall be concerned with developments in the Northern frontier.

Like John A. Macdonald, who had bound Canada together with a railway in the 1880s, and to whom he referred on every possible occasion, Diefenbaker spoke of new sinews of commerce to strengthen the nation, in this case "roads to resources," highways and railways which would link southern Canada to the billions of dollars worth of resources which presumably lay in the North, particularly the Provincial Norths, waiting to be exploited.

John Diefenbaker's "northern vision," like so many other episodes involving southern interest in northern Canada, inspired an enthusiasm that burned brightly, but briefly. The press and the public responded with enthusiasm to his call for people to build on the country's essential nordicity, to capture the northern Eldorado, the riches which lay between them and the Pole. Since this was a Canadian episode, it would not be entirely a free-enterprise crusade; the federal government was willing to do its part, particularly in building the necessary transportation and communications infrastructure.

In the long run, though, the northern vision proved to be, as the cliché of the political news commentators puts it, more sizzle than steak. There were a few initiatives, particularly in the Territorial North, such as the beginning of the Dempster Highway, which was eventually to link the Mackenzie Delta by road with the rest of the continent, and the development of Dawson City as a tourist attraction. But it did not have much effect in the Provincial Norths, which had less public glamour than the territories, and Diefenbaker could or would not translate the vision into real action. His appointment in 1960 of the notably uncharismatic Walter Dinsdale as minister of northern affairs to replace Alvin Hamilton (who had been an enthusiast for the idea), when what was needed was another Clifford Sifton for the North, showed that he was more interested in the northern vision as a rhetorical device for getting votes than as a plan of action. Within a few years of his triumph of 1958 his personal peculiarities were beginning to help drag his government towards its eventual defeat, and he had lost interest in the North.

Diefenbaker's "northern vision" campaign proved to be a side-show in the history and development of northern Canada. Nevertheless, the development which he preached did occur, though, with some exceptions, not as a result of the efforts of his government. What really sparked the growth of the Provincial Norths was the tremendous expansion of the world economy that occurred after 1945, both to service the demands of the cold war, and even more to satisfy the unprecedented demand for consumer goods that was such a marked feature of the "baby boom" era. The combination of a tremendous growth in the consumer market along with continuing high military expenditures led to an increased demand for raw materials. This in turn meant that regions with resources once considered commercially unprofitable because they were so far from markets were now economically viable. This expansion, which was global in scale, washed over the Provincial Norths, which had the added attraction to investors of being in an island of stability in the midst of a highly turbulent world.

Some provinces fostered their own "northern visions," though these, like Diefenbaker's, tended to be the results of a single person's enthusiasm rather than of a coherent government policy. Duff Pattullo in British Columbia is one example; another was Joe Phelps, minister of natural resources in Tommy Douglas's C.C.F. (now N.D.P.) government in Saskatchewan at the end of World War II. Phelps wished to develop the economy of northern Saskatchewan with a view to alleviating the poverty of its Native inhabitants, to improve the management of the provincial forests (which were in danger of being entirely exhausted of valuable timber), and to diversify the provincial economy away from agriculture through public investment. To these ends he set up three public corporations in northern Saskatchewan, marketing agencies for fur, fish, and timber. These corporations soon became the means by which a social democratic government could exercise control over the use of natural resources by private enterprise, and the Timber Board became highly controversial in the province. In 1971 the Blakeney government established a separate ministry for the province's North — the Department of Northern Saskatchewan. But after ten years of political controversy and charges of mismanagement, it was dismantled in 1982 by the new Conservative administration of Grant Devine.

The governments of Manitoba and Ontario also set up separate departments of northern affairs, but unlike the Saskatchewan department, which was responsible for the delivery of nearly all government services to the Provincial North, the Manitoba department, established in 1974, has its mandate restricted to the development of local government, and only in the most remote parts of the region, while the Ontario Ministry of Northern Affairs, established in 1977, serves the function of co-ordinating the northern activities of other ministries, and co-ordinating federal-provincial agreements that deal with northern Ontario. The government of Quebec considers its north to be principally that area covered by the James Bay and Northern Quebec Agreement; thus the agency most relevant to its Provincial North is the Secrétariat des Activités gouvernementals en milieu Amerindien et Inuit. British Columbia does not have a department of northern affairs, or even a department which is concerned primarily with its Provincial North. Alberta has established the Northern Alberta Development Corporation, and Newfoundland a Department of Rural Agricultural and Northern Development, to deal with the Provincial Norths of those two provinces.

The pace of northern development was also influenced by the availability of new technology, particularly a series of innovations which helped overcome the main liabilities of northern life (in the eyes of southerners) — distance, isolation, and cold. Nothing had a more dramatic effect on the development of the mining industry in the Provincial Norths than the airplane, since it greatly widened the area a prospector could cover in a season, and made it possible for supplies to be flown in to remote lakes. It also made it far easier for geologists to study the general features of large areas. Planes were more efficient than land transport in every way; one plane, for example, could easily supply a number of prospecting parties at the same time. The planes were so obviously a boon to the industry that they were adopted across the country almost as soon as they proved that they could be reliable carriers. Some mining companies ran their own air service, while others depended on private firms. As early as 1925, a float plane from Prince Rupert, British Columbia, was supplying prospectors in the Dease-Liard region. In the mid 1920s freight, passenger, and mail services were established in all the Provincial Norths, though most of the independent operators ran into trouble at the beginning of the depression, and many were absorbed by larger competitors; after 1931, when the price of gold rose sharply, business for the small carriers boomed again. By 1926, for example, two companies were flying between the railway at Sioux Lookout (where the Elliot brothers had developed special skis for landing planes on snow) and Minaki, Ontario into the mining camp of Red Lake, Laurentide Air was flying into Rouyn, Quebec, and Northern Aerial Mining Exploration was supplying Flin Flon, Manitoba.

Improvements in transportation, particularly the introduction of jet airplanes, helped tie the Provincial Norths into the national transportation network. Northern communities, once dependent on the skill of bush-pilots, now had regularly scheduled commercial flights to the south. The snowmobile, first marketed by J. A. Bombardier in 1937 and perfected after the war, revolutionized winter freight transport to remote communities, and his introduction of the Ski-Doo in 1959 did the same thing for personal transportation. Improvements in radio broadcast technology, and especially the spread of television in the 1960s, meant that northerners were no longer relegated to the conceptual sidelines of North American life, even though many communities in the North got their TV delayed on tape for many years until the launching of the Anik satellite in 1972. In the space of a single generation a sophisticated communications network spread across the Provincial Norths, overcoming the region's isolation and providing direct and immediate contact with the southern provinces and the rest of the world.

There was also a great expansion in highway transportation in the region in this period. In British Columbia, the pro-development Social Credit government of W. A. C. Bennett completed the Hart Highway, linking Prince George to Dawson Creek, and undertook the long-delayed work on extending the Pacific Great Eastern Railway (renamed The B.C. Railway) which extended it to Prince George in 1956 and Fort Nelson in 1971, giving the province a north-south link. Other railways — through northern Alberta to the Pine Point Mine in the N.W.T., the line to Schefferville, and the lines linking the new properties in northern Manitoba — were also built in this period, all with large infusions of public money. A maze of local access roads was built through the region for loggers, prospectors, and geologists looking for oil deposits.

In the same period, improvements in building and industrial design and heating technology added to the physical comfort of northern life. At the end of World War II, most northern buildings were copies of southern models, heated by wood-burning stoves which consumed huge quantities of cord wood. The advent of rock-wool and fibreglass insulation made northern buildings warmer and cheaper to heat. Yet the benefits of this technology were unevenly distributed, since Native housing remained distinctly substandard, and there was little attempt to change the basic concept of housing design to suit northern conditions. While the Nordic countries experimented with row housing and solar heating, the towns of the Provincial Norths simply replicated southern patterns: Thompson's houses were much like those of Winnipeg, Sudbury's like those of Toronto. This was only to be expected, since house design and construction in the region for the non-indigenous population was left largely to private enterprise, which had no impetus to do other than replicate southern models. Making northern towns as much as possible like southern ones probably made them more attractive to potential residents, as did the combination of improved travel and telecommunications.

Rhetoric, northern visions, television, and warm houses were not, however, sufficient to ensure a future of growth and prosperity for the Provincial Norths. The great issue for the region was its economic viability. Since the early days of this country the Provincial and Territorial Norths had often failed in this respect. The great example was the Klondike gold rush, which had not sustained its prosperity, and the story of the Klondike was illustrative of other places in northern British Columbia and the other northern provinces. And although some resource towns, notably in northern Ontario — Sudbury, Timmins, New Liskeard, Kirkland Lake — were close to forty years old, or older, by the end of the Second World War, the problem for the region as a whole was that there were not enough of them, and that they were scattered widely in a vast land. The sorry truth was that the Provincial Norths, for all their wealth and untapped resources, were not unusually rich in relation to their area. The pockets of heavily mineralized ground, the miles of timber, the rivers waiting to be dammed — they were all there, just as the promoters promised, but they were often remote, expensive to develop, and too often, except for the rivers, impermanent. As Canadians ventured into the region after 1945, they did so with a mixture of hope and reservation, the belief that wealth might be found, but with the realization that failure was entirely possible. It was this that led industry to request, or demand, that the government assist in development schemes.

The economic development of the new Provincial Norths rested on four economic elements: mining, forestry, hydro-electricity, and government expenditures, particularly in the areas of social programs and infrastructure. In the mining sector, the post-war era saw a shift from the specialized, high-grade properties of the past, particularly gold and silver, to an expanding interest in base metals and lower grade properties. An example was the remarkable development of the iron ore deposits in the interior of central Labrador in the late 1940s. This was a massive project, involving a new townsite, Schefferville (just across the provincial boundary in Quebec), the development of large open pit mines, and the construction at a cost of $250 million ($1 billion in 1992 dollars) of the Quebec, North Shore, and Labrador railway 600 km to the St. Lawrence River at Sept-Îles. By 1956 twelve million tons of ore were being delivered to the steel mills, and other iron ore properties were being developed at Wabush and Labrador City (in Labrador). Southwest of Wabush was developed the Quebec town of Gagnon, connected by a 300 km railway to Port Cartier on the St. Lawrence.

The history of Schefferville encapsulated one important aspect of the modern history of the Provincial Norths. Founded in 1953 (and given its name by Premier Maurice Duplessis in memory of Lionel Scheffer, first bishop of Labrador), it was the first organized municipality in Nouveau Québec, with a population that rose above 3,000. It produced as much as $270 million worth of iron ore in one year (1979), but by the early 1980s the mining operations on which the town depended had become unprofitable, and in 1983 they ceased, rendering Schefferville a virtual ghost town. It was simply the old boom and bust cycle on a larger scale. What made this episode particularly notable was that the president of the Iron Ore Company of Canada who pulled the plug on the town was Brian Mulroney. By all accounts his delivery of the death blow to the town was a political tour de force. Armed with charts and blarney, he told the community residents that revenues had fallen and that the company could no longer afford the expense of operating in such a remote region, and announced generous severance and relocation programs; the residents took the money and scattered to other mining towns. Mulroney emerged from the process with his reputation relatively untarnished — no mean feat considering that he had just announced the economic doom of an entire region.

In the 1950s it seemed that a mega-project was launched every year somewhere in the Provincial Norths. The huge aluminum smelter and power generating plant constructed at the beginning of the decade at Kitimat is an example (though Kitimat is at best on the periphery of the region). In the far north of Manitoba the Sherritt-Gordon Company began in 1951 to develop a nickel-copper deposit at Lynn Lake. An even larger development in northern Manitoba was Inco's mine at Thompson, which grew from nothing in 1956 to a city of 20,000 in ten years. Thompson had the good fortune to be located near the existing Hudson Bay Railway; it had the bad fortune, like the other mining towns, of being totally dependent for its prosperity on world prices for nickel. Unlike Schefferville, however, Thompson reached a size (14,300 in 1981) that guaranteed its survival even in bad times, if only as a regional service centre.

Saskatchewan's mineral boom town of the 1950s was a product of cold war defence policy. After 1945 the United States military-industrial complex developed an insatiable demand for uranium oxide, and since there was a large deposit on the north shore of Lake Athabasca, Uranium City came into being in 1952 to service the Eldorado and other mines there. The town grew to more than 2,500, but the waning of the cold war and a world glut of uranium led Eldorado to suspend operations in 1981, and the town died. Like Schefferville, it was simply too remote to sustain any role other than frontier boom town.

Northern Ontario already had many mining towns by 1945, but it also sprouted a new one, Elliot Lake, 140 km west of Sudbury. Founded in 1955, it served a number of uranium mines in the region, and within four years had 25,000 people. The Elliot Lake and Uranium City districts together produced almost all of Canada's $330 million worth of uranium ore in 1959. The history of Elliot Lake, like that of so many resource towns in the Provincial Norths, is that of boom and bust, though shorter and sharper than most. The town came into existence because of the cold war, when a seemingly insatiable demand for uranium ore to feed the American nuclear industry led to a frantic development of mining properties in a number of places. The Elliot Lake deposit was found accidentally when, in 1948, two prospectors casually passed their newly-acquired geiger counter over a collection of rocks on the desk of the Sault Ste. Marie mining recorder. The instrument clicked encouragingly, and the men set out to find the source of the rock.

Like much of the history of hard-rock mining discoveries in the Provincial Norths, this one would not have been possible without an extensive infrastructure of support stretching over many years. In the case of Elliot Lake, locating the actual deposit would have been almost impossible without the work of the Geological Survey of Canada, which had made a thorough survey of the region in 1925.

By 1953 the area from which the tell-tale rock had come had been well explored, and in the summer of that year a consortium staked 1,400 claims covering 56,000 acres. When the news of this activity got out, there was a rush to the area, and a further 8,000 claims were staked. Several mining properties were developed, the largest — the Denison mine — operated the biggest uranium mill in the world, processing 6,000 tons of ore per day.

Elliot Lake was carefully planned to be a community of 20 to 30,000 people. Fortunately for the planners and builders, the mining properties lay 30 to 50 kilometres from the Trans-Canada highway, though it was some of the most difficult terrain in the country for roads, as the builders of the Canadian Pacific Railway had discovered seventy years earlier. Very quickly a road was brought in from the main highway, and a pleasant townsite was laid out — "an aesthetically-pleasing community, built for permanence, unlike some other communities in Northern Ontario ... that had sprung up as an adjunct to industrial development." The result was "an outstanding example of large-scale planning and co-operation between government and private industry." When the Canadian government secured a contract with the U.S. Atomic Energy Commission for more than $1 billion worth of Elliot Lake uranium by 1963, the town's future seemed secure.

Almost immediately, however, the roof fell in on the community. There can be few towns in this country planned for permanence which began to shrink as quickly after their founding as did Elliot Lake. The problem was that it was vulnerable not only to changes in the world economy, but also to international politics. In this case, the culprit was the easing of the cold war, and a relatively saner approach to the arms race. In November 1959 the Americans announced that their domestic supplies of uranium were sufficient for their needs, and although the contracts would be honoured, they would buy no more from Canada. The alternative market for uranium was for generating electricity, but reactors which could use the town's output were a number of years in the future. Within a year five mines closed, and by 1965 the town had shrunk by 75 percent, to 6,600 residents.

Unlike other resource towns in a similar situation, Elliot Lake had the great advantage of being in a relatively southern location, a short day's drive from Toronto; it was also helpful after the Liberals came to power in Ottawa in 1964, that the region's MP was Prime Minister Lester Pearson. Government found a variety of uses for Elliot Lake and its mines. A research centre was established at one mining property, and part of another was taken over and used by the provincial department of reform institutions. A nuclear and mining museum was built in the town, along with a government centre for continuing education. One mine, the Rio Algom, was able to continue to export uranium ore to the United Kingdom, and the Canadian government kept the large Denison Mine open by buying its output and stockpiling it.

Elliot Lake's fortunes improved in the 1970s, with contracts to supply nuclear generating plants in Japan and in Canada, particularly the station at Pickering, outside Toronto, which began producing electricity in 1971. In 1978 Ontario promised to buy enough uranium from Elliot Lake to support a community of 30,000 until the year 2020. Then new storm clouds rolled in. The nuclear electric industry, which had been touted in the 1950s and 1960s as the technological and economic miracle of the late twentieth century, collapsed in a tangle of government regulations, cost overruns, and accusations of danger to the public. Electricity "too cheap to meter" — the boast of the 1950s — became a cruel joke. All uranium towns suffered, and Elliot Lake was particularly vulnerable because its product was by the 1970s more expensive than uranium mined elsewhere, particularly in Saskatchewan.

In 1991 Ontario Hydro announced that it would stop buying Elliot Lake uranium. Furious lobbying by the town's mayor, who was also the head of the union local, won a new promise of a $250 million package which will employ 575 miners until 1995 (at their peak the local mines employed nearly 7,500). Its more southerly location, contracts from Ontario Hydro's nuclear generating plants, and subsidies from the province have so far kept the town alive. It was significant that the Ontario NDP government's announcement that Elliot Lake would be kept alive at public expense was greeted with some degree of public outrage in the province. Ontarians were not troubled by the transfer of millions of dollars' worth of resources from the northern part of the province to the benefit of southern consumers and the provincial treasury. When the idea was mooted that the process might work in reverse — that the uranium industry might be subsidized through hard times by means of purchases by Ontario Hydro of uranium at artificially high prices — there was consternation.

The town also turned to alternate sources of strength. The most successful has been the Retirement Living Program, a scheme that began in 1987 to fill houses vacated by departing citizens with retirees from Toronto and southern Ontario, attracted by low rents, modern facilities, and a quiet life. In the first year of the plan, 29 residential units were rented, in the next year 350, and 300 more in 1989. The proportion of the town's population over 65 climbed from less than 2 percent to more than 10 percent, and is expected to triple again by 1993.

Elliot Lake now has a population of 13,000, and its future as a kind of Sun City North seems secure. This is cold comfort, however, to the thousands of miners and their families who were forced to pack up and leave, in an exodus all too familiar in that transient industry. Nor does it serve as a useful example for more remote communities. There has been no great influx of retirees from Montreal to Schefferville, for instance, nor from Regina to Uranium City, and the decline of Cassiar, British Columbia, whose doom was sealed by the closing of its asbestos mine in February 1992 and the refusal of the British Columbia government to keep it alive, seems irreversible.

Northern Alberta and British Columbia experienced a boom in natural gas production in the post-war years. Unlike mining, the production of natural gas did not require the establishment of towns; the major infrastructure other than wells was a network of underground pipelines, which once in place needed little maintenance. Thus the tremendous discoveries in the Swan Hills, Rainbow, and Zama regions of Alberta and the smaller fields in northern British Columbia did not result in the mushrooming growth of instant cities, though the towns already in existence such as Fort St. John and Fort Nelson did prosper as a result of the nearby exploration and construction activity. The development of the enormous deposits of petroleum in the northern Alberta tar sands — 100 million cubic metres in the Ft. McMurray deposit alone — has the potential to be the Provincial North's Eldorado of the twenty-first century, if the world price of petroleum goes high enough to make the deposits pay. The first modern plant for extracting oil from the sands began production in 1967, and a second, Syncrude, opened in 1978, produces nearly 19,000 cubic metres per day.

Gold, which had been the mainstay of Canada's northern mining industry earlier in the century, was troubled at the end of World War II. The price of gold was fixed during the 1930s by the United States at $35 an ounce, and since the U.S. had the economic power until the 1970s to enforce this price, Canadian producers were caught in a cost-price squeeze which threatened to devastate the industry. Relief came from Ottawa in the form of the Gold Mining Assistance Act of 1947, which subsidized the production of gold, and kept the gold-mining towns like Kirkland Lake and Timmins alive. When the declining economic influence of the U.S. led to a freeing of gold prices in the early 1970s, the price rose briefly to $800 an ounce, leading to a tremendous rush of prospecting and development, and although the price soon fell by half, Canada was still the world's third largest producer of gold in 1983, with an output valued at $1.3 billion, most of it coming from the Provincial Norths — a quarter from northern Ontario alone.

The coal development at Tumbler Ridge, British Columbia is a more recent example of the pattern of economic development in the Provincial Norths. It was not begun to serve a general world commodity market for coal, but was directed specifically at Japanese industry, which was believed in the 1970s to have an insatiable demand for coal, and would pay high prices for it. The project became the cornerstone of the provincial government's plan for the development of the North in the 1970s, and attracted hundreds of millions of dollars of development. The entire Northeast Coal Project, of which the Tumbler Ridge operations were a part, required a total investment of $4.5 billion, to which the federal and provincial governments contributed a third. However, price fluctuations and international competition made the project much less of a bonanza, showing once more the risks inherent in mega-projects, and the vulnerability of the region to forces beyond its control.

The other great engine of wealth in the Provincial Norths after World War II was a greatly expanded forest industry. Much of this growth — the result of the tremendous pent-up demand for housing and consumer goods after fifteen years of depression and war — was sustained and healthy, bringing growth and prosperity to northern and northwestern Ontario, northern British Columbia, Saskatchewan, and Quebec. What happened to the industry in northern Manitoba, however, was a cautionary tale which revealed "how many pitfalls could lie in the path of an unsophisticated government eager to encourage resource development." Eager to get in on what seemed like a sure thing for northern development, the government of Manitoba contracted with a Swiss company to build a large lumber and pulp and paper complex at The Pas. The result, Churchill Forest Industries, was begun under the Conservatives in 1966 and put in receivership by the NDP in 1971 after an undetermined number of millions of dollars had been siphoned off by foreign companies. Although the complex was completed, it was so heavily burdened by debt that it remained an embarrassment for the province rather than a triumph of northern development.

Other towns fared better. Thunder Bay and Kenora in Ontario, Prince George in British Columbia and Prince Albert, Saskatchewan, all grew rapidly after the war as lumber and pulp and paper mills were built to serve a booming North American market. All four towns had good rail service, and all became local but important centres of industrial prosperity in the 1950s and 1960s, the characteristic sulphuric smell of the mills cheerfully described by civic boosters as "the smell of money." The forestry industry was able to give the Provincial Norths something that mining had not — long-term stability, as well as value-added jobs within the region. The industry is not immune to international economic cycles, nor to the depletion of resources, but it does not fluctuate as violently as does mining, and its towns, though they have ups and downs, do not become ghost towns. The greatest threat to these towns in the late 1980s was not falling prices, but environmental regulations and technology. Employment in the forests themselves has been greatly affected by technology, as legions of wood-cutters have been largely replaced by machines which cut and strip the trees, and can turn them into chips, all on site. Those mills that were notorious polluters or were inefficient users of labour — most notably the older mills in Ontario and Quebec — have had a very difficult time competing, and some of them have closed. New developments have had to prove that they will not damage the environment, something that given the nature of the industry is not easy to do. The most notable recent example of these difficulties was the proposal for a tremendous development of pulp mills in northern Alberta funded by Japanese capital. This proposal entailed $4.5 billion worth of capital investment; the largest stake would be held by Alberta-Pacific Forest Products ($1.3 b.) and Daishowa Canada ($1.2 b.), and the total timber lease would be over 150,000 km^2. The provincial government jumped at the chance to diversify the provincial economy, and participated with the federal government in promises of loans to the companies and $75 million worth of roads and rail lines to the new mills. But environmentalists, Native organizations, and the government of the Northwest Territories, appalled by the possibility of damage to the Peace River–Lake Athabasca drainage region, mounted an attack on the plan which has delayed it. The companies have promised that new industrial processes will be less polluting, however, and the Alberta government remains determined to go ahead with a revised plan.

Perhaps the most dramatic, or at least the best-publicized aspect of the current economic development of the Provincial Norths is in hydro-electric dams, because they are clean, sup-posedly non-polluting, require no large towns in the region, and because the wealth that they produce will flow "as long as the rivers run." Yet of course they can do great environmen-tal damage; though they leave the air clean, they can destroy the land, and often, ironically, the wealth that flows from them causes the rivers in fact to stop running altogether. The hydro frontier came to the region fifty years ago, but it still is the bright shining hope, not of northern prosperity, but of the prosperity that the North is supposed to bring to the south — an old but apparently imperishable concept. Three examples give the flavour of the successes and perils of this old yet modern dream.

The first is the unhappy experience of the province of Newfoundland. One of Premier Joey Smallwood's many dreams for the financial betterment of his province was the development of hydro-electric power in the basin of the Churchill river in Labrador (originally the Hamilton river, but re-named by Smallwood, who admired the British prime minister). To bring the electricity to the potential customers in the United States, high-voltage transmission lines had to be built across Quebec. In order to secure Quebec's permission and raise the nearly $1 billion that the project would cost, Smallwood had to contract to sell most of the power to Hydro-Québec at 0.3 cents per kwh for a 40-year period, and 0.2 cents for another 25 years. The project was built (1967–1974), but Newfoundland received only a pittance from it, while Hydro-Québec resold much of the power to the Americans at a huge profit, especially after the energy crisis of the 1970s sent the price of power zooming. Newfoundland's attempts in court and in the political arena to secure better terms have been totally unsuccessful, and the project remains a painful reminder to the province of opportunities lost in its Provincial North.

British Columbia's great northern hydro project was initiated by W. A. C. Bennett, like Smallwood a charismatic leader tending to run a one-man show, but unlike Smallwood not dependent on another province for the success of his dream. Bennett, although ostensibly a free-enterpriser, had expropriated the province's largest hydro-electric firm in 1961, and created B.C. Hydro to develop the province's power potential. The great northern scheme was a dam on the Peace River near Hudson's Hope, eventually named the W. A. C. Bennett Dam. Its generating stations, built 1968–1980, produce more than 3 million megawatts annually, but the curtailment of the flow of the Peace River had a serious effect on the wetlands of the river's delta at Lake Athabasca which is only now becoming evident, leading to a continuing controversy.

Nowhere, however, has hydro-electric development in the Provincial Norths been more closely identified with provincial (some would say national) aspirations than in Quebec. The process was first mooted in the 1960s, when René Lévesque was minister of natural resources in the government of Jean Lesage. Lévesque believed that hydro-electric development would give Quebec the financial power and industrial resources to take control of its economy away from the English-speaking developers who had dominated it for generations. The centrepiece of Quebec's aspirations was the James Bay Project, the largest civil engineering work ever undertaken in North America, involving the construction of dams, diversions of rivers, creation of lakes, and the expenditure of $15 billion. The power was to be used for Quebec industry (aluminum smelters, for example), and for export to the United States, for whom Quebec would become to electricity what Saudi Arabia was to oil. Actual construction was announced by Premier Robert Bourassa in 1971. Unfortunately, the tremendous reshaping of the James Bay region was bound to inflict great damage on the traditional lands of the Cree who lived in the region, and who had not been consulted about it, or even notified that it was about to take place. Given the fact that no treaty had even been signed with them for the extinguishment of their aboriginal rights, this was at worst unforgivable and at best politically foolish on the part of the Quebec government.

The battle of the James Bay Cree, led by Chief Billy Diamond, to secure compensation for the damage done by the project, resulted in the first comprehensive Native claim to be settled in Canada. The James Bay agreement of 1975 gave the Cree $225 million and other compensation, but their main community, Fort George, was uprooted and moved, much of their traditional trapping land was drowned, and a number of social ills accompanied the access road built to the new community of Chisasibi. Not surprisingly, the announcement of the second phase of the project in the late 1980s renewed the struggle. This phase of the project calls for five power stations with a generating capacity equal to 20 percent of Canada's total hydro-electric output, and the creation of reservoirs equal to half the size of Lake Ontario. Something so huge will have a dramatic effect on the environment of the region, and an alliance of Native and environmental groups is currently attempting to delay it. Less well known, but equally vital to the people in the region is the struggle over a proposed hydro-electric development plan in the basin of Ontario's Moose River. Recently the Moose River Band joined the Manitoba Cree and the James Bay Cree to present a united front against energy development in all three Provincial Norths.

Hydro-electric development, which seems so modern, is actually an updated version of a very old theme in the Provincial Norths: the colonization of the region in which the resource wealth flows out of it to the south, while the damage remains in the North. Imagine another scenario, in which government announces that the profits from hydro development will be reinvested in the North and used for industrialization and other benefits for Northerners. This redistribution of wealth would produce thousands of jobs in the region, provide economic stability, and would increase the economic and political power of Northerners. It is also a pipe dream, one which would seem ludicrous to most Canadians, proving not that it is a foolish idea, but that the national attitude towards the region seems fixed in stone.

For the Native people of the Provincial Norths, the advent of the new industrial age brought sweeping changes. As late as 1945, most of the indigenous peoples of the region, particularly those not connected by road or rail with the south, still lived on the land, hunting for subsistence and trapping for cash, a successful and sustainable adaptation to their location on the margins of the Euro-Canadian industrialized world. It provided them with the goods and products that they wanted, while leaving them essentially free to pursue traditional cultural and social activities. While those who lived near areas of settlement faced some pressure from missionaries and government officials to conform to mainstream values, those in the more remote regions were generally left alone.

Much of this changed after 1945 as first the resource frontier, then the welfare frontier, and finally what might be called the environmentalist frontier advanced upon the Native people. The net effect was a profound transformation of aboriginal life, the destabilization of indigenous culture — particularly language and the authority of elders — and a rapid decline in traditional knowledge.

The chief engine of this change was a process which has been called "welfare colonialism." Students of the entire process of colonialism have noted a qualitative shift in the actions of colonial authorities after World War II. Whereas earlier colonial systems involved the subjugation of indigenous peoples, typically by force, and the exploitation of their lands and resources, the new form of colonialism was liberal and benevolent, predicated on the assumption that indigenous peoples should be rapidly moved towards assimilation into the nation. Sparked by a seeming generosity, and apparently free of racism (at least the classic forms of it), this colonialism nevertheless did much harm to the people it was ostensibly designed to help.

In his 1977 study *The White Arctic*, Robert Paine wrote of welfare colonialism,

> Any decision taken by the colonizers has a basic flaw: a decision made for the material benefit of the colonized at the same time can be construed as disadvantaging them; a "generous" or "sensible" decision can be at the same time morally "wrong." This is so because it is the colonizers who make the decisions that control the future of the colonized; because the decisions are made (ambiguously) on behalf of the colonized, and yet in the name of the colonizers' culture (and of their political, administrative and economic priorities).

Faced with the dismal living conditions of many (but by no means all) indigenous peoples, and imbued with the political rhetoric of egalitarianism and equality, liberal-minded governments launched a flotilla of programs to improve their standard of living.

Equating assimilationism with equality and respect for indigenous people revealed the basic flaw of welfare colonialism. However much its practitioners claimed to be charting a new and kinder course, most of it reflected the values and ideology of the dominant society. The programs may have been new, and many, and certainly they were expensive, but they maintained the earlier pattern of attempting to draw Native people into the national mainstream — indeed, this was the stated purpose of the short-lived White Paper of the Trudeau government, floated in 1969, but hurriedly withdrawn under a barrage of Native protest. If there was an inherent contradiction between the new liberal agenda, with its programs for education, housing, economic development, and all kinds of social assistance on one hand, and what the Native people of the Provincial Norths themselves may have wanted, it was not readily apparent to the policy-makers and social engineers. Failures in these programs were often attributed to the shortcomings of the client groups, and not to the structural or ideological limitations of welfare colonialism.

It would be wrong, however, to dismiss the attempts of the post-war era to ameliorate the lives of the Native people of the Provincial Norths out of hand. Developments such as dramatically improved medical care, especially a campaign against tuberculosis and a program of community-based public health, improved their lives, and the advent of evacuation by plane or helicopter for the seriously ill meant for the first time that medical care for the small communities in the region at least approached that of the cities in southern Canada. Whatever the failings of the education system were, and they were many, it did produce a generation of Native leaders with the skills and the knowledge to challenge the government and industry and to fight with increasing success in the 1970s and 1980s for Native rights. Those who promoted these plans argued with some justice that the government had only moved into a gap left by the collapse of the traditional Native economy, and brought the indigenous people the health and the tools to adapt to changing times.

Because social engineering is based as much on faith — how one views society and societal obligations — as on fact and statistics, it is as difficult to come to a final judgement on the programs of welfare colonialism (Would the Native People have been "best left as Indians"? Was the government making the best of a bad situation?) as it is to assess the merits of different religious faiths. The programs undoubtedly brought benefits to the people they served, and it is hard to argue that it would have been better had government done nothing at all. But there certainly are plenty of horror stories to support the view of those who believe that the era was one of thoughtless meddling in the lives of indigenous people that caused tremendous damage. The residents of the Grassy Narrows reserve in northwestern Ontario, for instance, were compelled to move from one side of the river to the other to make it easier to supply them with the services of the welfare state. They subsequently found themselves victims of social pathologies stemming from a sense of lost community, combined with mercury poisoning from a pulp mill which discharged its effluent into the river from which they caught the fish that were their main food supply. This is but one item on a long sad list of damaged indigenous communities. The residents of Chisasibi, the central community of the James Bay Cree, linked to the south in the 1970s by a road built to service the James Bay hydro project — these people are another.

The causes of social disruption seem easy enough to explain on one level, but there are many difficult questions even here. Did the collapse of aboriginal languages originate in the residential and day schools, or was it a consequence of the advent of mass culture through radio and television? How does one explain, let alone quantify, the declining authority of Native elders, and the weakening of family and tribal systems of social control? Did the end of living on the land result in less attention to other aspects of Native culture such as traditional medicines and methods of healing, or was it the authority attached to the non- Natives who intervened in their lives that killed the old ways? Is the abuse of alcohol and other drugs a cause or a symptom of social distress?

On another level, the cost of the government's paternalism cannot be measured entirely by houses built in Native communities or the educational achievement of Native students. It must also be measured in the degree to which these programs stripped indigenous people of the power of self-determination, removing from them the right to make even the most basic decisions — how to educate their children, how to spend money, and even where to live. Nor did the mega-projects of the 1960s and 1970s bring much prosperity to these people, although developers often promised to hire Native workers, and some training programs were set up for them. The government programs tended to be excellent employment programs, but not for the Natives — the jobs went to the professionals who were trained to help them.

The years after 1950 therefore saw two assaults on the indigenous economy. Falling prices for pelts devastated the fur trade; though prices eventually rebounded, the animal rights movement of the 1980s dealt it another serious blow with a successful international boycott of Canadian fur products. Secondly, the expanding exploitation of resources has slowly eroded the food base on which many of the indigenous people continue to rely — the James Bay project is the best known but certainly not the only example; the activities of Manitoba Hydro in the north of that province, for instance, have had a similar effect on the Native people there. This economic squeeze occurred at a time when the welfare state was expanding rapidly, so there were programs designed to fill the gap left by the decline of traditional activities. The family allowance, the old age pension, training grants, grants for band councils, grants for cultural activities, grants for broadcasting, newspapers and many other activities — all were eagerly accepted by the Native people. They then increasingly found themselves dependent on them. The Native economy in general had changed from a traditional one based on the land to one based on the bounty of the welfare state, supplemented by occasional wage labour and the declining returns from the land. By then the word "unemployment" began to mean something in Native communities. In 1900 the "unemployment rate" in a community like Pukatawagan in north-eastern Manitoba would have been close to 100 percent, since no one there had a "job," yet such a statement means nothing, certainly not as an indicator of social distress. But if the unemployment rate there or in a community like it today is 80 percent, everyone knows what that means, as a rule — alcoholism, violence, suicide, school drop-outs, and all the rest of the sad litany of social pathology. Many young people, the men in particular, spend much of their lives in jail, victims of what is to them an alien justice system as much as of the social problems of their communities. All of this misery, added to the economic and cultural difficulties, only increased the conviction of paternalists that Native people are incapable of managing their own affairs, and the spiral of dependency winds deeper and deeper.

It is easy to diagnose the disease, but much less easy to prescribe a cure, especially under the present economic structure of the Provincial Norths vis-à-vis the rest of the country. The indigenous communities of the Provincial Norths face a harsh reality: they have been penetrated by the modern industrial system just far enough to destroy or damage their own system, but not far enough to bring them all of its benefits; in particular, they are simply too remote to be able to participate in the contemporary economic system, except as wards of it. Some communities have been fortunate enough — though it is a distinctly mixed blessing — to have a forestry operation, a mine, or a hydro project located nearby. If the project operators are well-disposed to Native employees, which is not always the case, or if some level of government compels them to employ Natives as a condition of granting permission for the project, which happens increasingly often, then there is the prospect of steady work and economic advancement. But most Native communities — from Telegraph Creek, British Columbia, to Summer Beaver, Ontario, to Nain in Labrador — are too far from centres of economic activity to have much of a commercial future. Non-Native people have traditionally dealt with this situation by leaving the community and the region; some Native people have done the same thing, though as often as not for social as much as economic reasons, and have moved to cities. It is for this reason that it was observed recently in the press that Toronto has become the "largest Native reserve in Canada," though Winnipeg, Regina, and Vancouver might contest the title. For those who choose to remain, there are few economic alternatives to welfare payments.

The reality is that since the 1950s, Native people in the Provincial Norths have had few economic options. The fur trade has declined, food hunting had dwindled, partly because of the harm done to the environment by outsiders, but also because young people have lost interest in following their elders onto the land, and jobs for wages are few. The necessities of life are purchased with welfare payments, a system which dampens the morale of the people. There have been many efforts to rectify this situation, typically reflecting the belief that the solution lies in Native entrepreneurship. There have been some successes, such as the investments made by the James Bay Cree in their airline, Air Creebec, and in other projects. The people of the Metis settlement of Paddle Prairie, Alberta, purchased a local gas station and shopping complex through a community-wide share holding, and operate the facility to the benefit of the community. But long-term successes of this sort are all too few, for the limitations of small and uncertain markets, the distance from suppliers, the high costs of working in sub-Arctic conditions, and episodes of bad management add extra burdens to already marginal operations.

Because Native society has shown a greater resilience than the doomsayers of the last century would have admitted, it would be a brave and foolish forecaster who would predict that the decline of indigenous cultures is total or irreversible. Yet it is obvious that virtually every Native group in the Provincial Norths has experienced profound disruptions, and a loss of traditional culture and values. Some indigenous languages are shrinking or in actual danger of disappearing, and in some communities almost no one under the age of forty speaks them. An immeasurable quantity of traditional knowledge has died with elders who could not find young people interested in learning the old ways. Traditional means of social control have almost disappeared in some places, though in others they continue to operate, often behind the scenes. The federal government's insistence on the adoption of the elected chief and band council system of community government has stripped clan leaders and elders of their traditional positions of authority, transferring power to younger, more assimilated leaders who are better trained to deal with non-Native authorities.

Native people did not sit with their hands folded as these transformations occurred, but in many cases they have lacked the power to make changes in the agenda prescribed for them. Some of them struggled for years, with few resources and without attracting much publicity, to keep their cases before the courts and before government — the Nisga'a of northwestern British Columbia, who fought for their rights for decades before the modern era of land claims, are an excellent example. But through the 1950s and 1960s Native people found few supporters in southern Canada, and lacked the financial power to sustain a challenge to the status quo.

The backlash against the ill-conceived 1969 White Paper of the Trudeau government, which suggested that the solution to the problems of Native people was to do away with their separate status and treat them like other Canadians, along with a rising tide of social concern resulting perhaps from the culture of the 1960s, combined with the moral victory of the Nisga'a in the 1973 Calder Case (they lost on a technicality, but the case was the harbinger of the later comprehensive claims movement) to give new hope to Native people and a tremendous boost to the Native land claims process. At the same time, they began to fight against the ravages of development.

The Natives of northern Manitoba, particularly those at Southern Indian Lake, stood up to Manitoba Hydro, demanding first the abandonment of the plan to flood their lands by damming the Nelson and Churchill Rivers, and later, redress for damage done their lands. A statement by Sidney Green, the minister in the Schreyer government responsible for the environment, showed how officials, even NDP politicians, weighed the interests of northern Natives against economic prosperity:

> While there are some who are bluntly opposed to the concept of so-called modern civilization and materialism, the Government of Manitoba feels it owes a responsibility to its citizens to proceed with intelligent development of our natural resources for the material benefit of our citizens ... society [must] consider a trade-off between maintenance of the ecology in its existing form and developing to the fullest the potential of our natural resource in accordance with value standards adopted by society. There is no question that the Nelson River Development will result in ecological changes. In our judgement the values to be obtained greatly overshadow the problems which will arise.

The Native people of Southern Indian Lake lost their fight to prevent the damage to their lands. When the James Bay Cree sought an injunction against the first stage of the James Bay

Hydro project, on the other hand, they won a victory which also helped launch the comprehensive claims movement. Some of these struggles have turned inward, and there have been charges of corruption directed against Native leaders, charges which often lead outsiders to suggest that Native people are not ready for self-government. In 1991 a group of Native women led a protest against the male-dominated Native leadership, claiming that women's concerns are not given sufficient attention in band council and tribal meetings. But such internal difficulties reflect the continued maturation of the Native political movement rather than inherent weaknesses — and for stories of corruption, read the history of any large American city in the nineteenth century; no one now suggests that Irish-Americans are incapable of self-government.

The confrontations over resource development on aboriginal lands in the Provincial Norths have come to symbolize much of the current history of the region, as well as the hopes for its future. Because so much money is involved in these projects, the controversies surrounding them carry an urgency which cannot be ignored, and the "Native People vs. developers" scenario plays much better on the television news than a more subtle debate about who should control the school system in a Native community.

One irony of the post-war era is that the development which brought so many problems to Native communities also made the Provincial Norths much more attractive to non-Native settlers. Traditionally, those moving into the region had to make considerable sacrifices in their way of life, and towns like The Pas, Rouyn, Timmins, and Smithers were pretty rough places, with few amenities. The company town of the post-war era helped change this, for in the boom years of the 1950s and 1960s, company managers discovered that workers and their families would not move into the North unless they were given a reasonably attractive place to live. Thus Labrador City, Schefferville, Kitimat, Thompson, Uranium City, Tumbler Ridge, Elliot Lake and the rest, were built with attractive homes at attractive prices, and a wide range of recreational facilities. The wages were generally high, and though attractive houses and a municipal swimming pool did not mean that the town would last any longer than the resources it depended on, at least while it existed it was more stable than similar towns in the past. It was not, however, in the historic sense a really northern community; it was more like a southern enclave, designed to attract people who would not otherwise consider living in the North.

Before 1945, living in a town in the Provincial Norths often meant doing without some services that were common in southern towns — whether it was a sanitation system, broadcast radio, roads to the south, or a regular supply of groceries (the farther north the town was, the more likely this tended to be). After 1960 it often meant living in a community which had better facilities per capita than southern towns.

Viewed from this perspective, it seems that the past decades have brought tremendous progress to the Provincial Norths. The signs are abundant: highways, railways, radio and television, schools, recreational and cultural facilities, airline service, thousands of new jobs in resource and service industries. But there has also been environmental degradation, and the transfer of wealth out of the region, which are the price that the residents of the region have paid to the rest of the country. Given the wealth that the region has produced, the returns have been meagre. Northern Manitoba has produced tremendous wealth for the province in minerals, forest products, and hydro-electricity, yet many of its Native communities lack proper housing, water and sanitation facilities, and have social problems that dwarf anything that exists in southern communities. Much the same is true across the region, for this is the reality of the colonization of the Provincial Norths. The resources have been identified and developed, an infrastructure completed, and a new social order imposed. This was done without the region gaining any sense of a trans-provincial identity. The protests, and there were many, were directed towards the provincial capitals, but for all of their common experiences, the Provincial Norths developed in this era without a common response to the imposed structures and controls of Canadian colonialism.

Chapter Six

Divided Dreams: Perspectives on the Modern Provincial North

Like the rest of Canada — for there is no reason that they should be any different — the Provincial Norths are in a rest-less and cranky mood as the twentieth century comes to its close. In the past twenty years the region has become a political and economic battle-ground where, as elsewhere, campaigns for public support and legal advantage are being waged, though up to the present the fighting has been largely in the media rather than on the streets. With a few widely publicized exceptions — Temagami, Lubicon Lake, northern British Columbia — physical confrontation and violence have not yet been a part of the struggle for the Provincial Norths, the struggle in which the dreams of the Native inhabitants increas-ingly clash with the visions of development-oriented newcom-ers. But Canadians should make no mistake about the potential for serious conflict inherent in these different visions of the contemporary North where Native people, numerically weak, but acquiring experience, skill, and political acumen daily, are mounting a struggle to prevent the continued despoliation of their homeland and the further dislocation of their cultures.

In the 1960s and 1970s, when Native communities in north-ern Manitoba, British Columbia, and particularly Quebec were disrupted by a series of mega-projects, a vigorous aboriginal protest movement was created. Yet few Canadians paid much attention to it. Through the efforts of groups such as Project North, an ecumenical church organization established in 1975 to help Native people in their struggles with those who seek to change the face of their lands, public consciousness of these issues has been raised to a considerable extent. But until quite recently the traditional ethos of the development and industrial expansion of the northern frontier has continued to be the norm. The James Bay Cree, for instance, did win a kind of victory when they delayed the James Bay project long enough to secure a land claim settlement; but this was the exception to the rule, and it was a Pyrrhic victory, for the project went ahead, causing many of the social and environmental problems that its critics predicted. Although indigenous people in the Yukon and Northwest Territories have been highly successful in this period in drawing political and public attention to their concerns, those of the Provincial Norths have had more difficulty in placing their problems on the national agenda.

The reasons for this are fairly straightforward. The main one is that in the Territories the federal government, which has constitutional responsibility for Native people, is far more powerful than in the provinces, where it shares power to a much greater extent with the regional government. In the Northwest Territories, for instance, Ottawa controls Crown lands and supplies 80 percent of Territorial revenue, which makes the Territorial government at Yellowknife a distinctly lesser player in land claims and other negotiations. This is not true in the provinces, which control their own Crown lands, supply far more of their own revenues, and must be dealt with as strong partners in negotiations. Another reason is that there is far more at stake for non-Natives in the northern provinces than in the Territories. It is one thing to turn over much of Baffin Island to the Inuit of Nunavut; for all the recent rhetoric about what a bargain Ottawa is getting for its millions in the pending Nunavut agreement, there is not an enormous economic stake in much of the region. The same is definitely not true of the northern provinces, where the stakes are vastly higher.

It is largely for these reasons — the much greater power of the provinces, and the economic importance of the Provincial Norths to the nation — that there are so many unresolved disputes in the region. Whether it is the gold property at Estay Creek in northwestern British Columbia, tar sands development near Fort McMurray Alberta, uranium prospects in northern Saskatchewan, forestry resources in northern Manitoba and Ontario, or hydro-electric power in northern Quebec (the financial foundation of the plans of Quebec separatists), northern resources stand at the forefront of development dreams, and thus at the centre of the future of Canadian prosperity. Little but the locale has changed since the time of Confederation, when visionaries posited a Canadian empire, based then on the wealth of the prairies, and now on the resources of the country's North.

If there is a difference, it is that the concerns of the Native groups cannot be swept aside as those of the Indians of the prairies were in the last century. The Innu trying to stop low-level flights over Labrador, the James Bay Cree's campaign against the second stage of the James Bay project in northern Quebec, the Teme-Augama Anishnabi joining with environmental organizations to block forestry activities in northern Ontario, the Cree of northern Manitoba demanding compensation for the damage caused to their land by hydro dam construction, the Lubicon of northern Alberta trying to secure provincial and federal agreement to their land claim, the Native people of northern British Columbia fighting on a number of fronts, notably Alcan's Kemano hydro-development project on the Nechako River — all have had some degree of success in bringing their cases to public attention, and all have had an influence over the public agenda that the Cree and Assiniboine of the 1870s could only dream of.

The process by which a nation bases an important part of its economy on the transfer of wealth and resources out of areas whose residents have very little control over the procedure bears a striking similarity to the French and British imperialism which shaped the early history of this country. Much as European interests developed Canadian resources for the benefit of England and France, the current pattern of northern development shifts the benefits to the south, while leaving the costs — social and cultural disruption, environmental damage — with the residents of the North. It is Vancouver, Calgary, Winnipeg, Toronto, Montreal that are the primary beneficiaries of northern development; it is there that the jobs are created and the financial benefits flow. Cheap electricity from northern Quebec, for example, is the foundation of that province's aluminum industry; northern electricity also benefits Manitoba and British Columbia, but in only a few places in the country — the aluminum smelter at Kitimat and the major pulp and paper towns are exceptions that prove the rule — do the jobs and other economic benefits stay in the region that produces the power.

But there is more to colonialism than the financial transfers resulting from resource development, though this process is at its core. Colonialism creates a certain way of thinking, one which makes the colonial region seem peripheral, unattractive, and even uninhabitable. Throughout our history, Canadian artists and writers have portrayed the North as a harsh and inaccessible place, a region of beautiful landscape but limited opportunities. The paintings of the Group of Seven, for instance, show a country which is majestic, but without human dimension. Most early southern observers not only ignored or denigrated Native inhabitants, but provided a picture of a region which seemed unsuitable for non-Native settlement. These images both reflected and reinforced the southern attitude that the North was a place to visit, do heroic deeds (as the continuing plethora of trek-across-the-wilderness books bears witness), or to make a short-term home while the money is good. The reality of northern life can be different, as the non-Natives who have chosen to make their permanent home there can attest, and as the Native people continue to demonstrate. But deeply ingrained national assumptions are difficult to change.

Attitudes to the North are thrown into sharp relief by economic crises, such as that faced by the residents of a single-industry town facing closure. Whether in Elliot Lake, Ontario, Schefferville, Quebec, or Uranium City, Saskatchewan, many residents come to develop a strong attachment to their community which goes beyond mere economics, and struggle to keep them alive in the face of inexorable pressures to shut them down and the indifference of people in the rest of the country. Brian Mulroney, when he was president of Iron Ore Canada, was only the most famous (and one of the most successful) among corporate executives who have rung the death knell for a company town and its residents. Sometimes the provincial governments will rush to save a dying northern community with a financial aid package, as in the case of Elliot Lake; at other times, as in the case of Uranium City, the community is allowed to die. Some towns try to attract other industries, government offices, or attempt to market themselves as holiday destinations — though rarely with the chutzpah of the British Columbia cabinet minister who suggested that clear-cut logging sites could be marketed as a tourist attractions. But unless the town has some other reason for existence than its single industry — unless it becomes, like The Pas and Thompson Manitoba, a regional resource and administrative centre — it is generally doomed. One of the messages these episodes send out is that there are some people who have tried the North and found they liked it, and that they resent their total dependence on outside commercial and economic forces over which they have no control whatsoever.

This cycle of birth and death has traditionally been the pattern of northern resource towns, but recently, proposals have been made to solve the problem by abolishing the northern company town altogether. The alternative would be fly-in camps. Workers would live in a nearby community, or in the closest metropolitan centre, and would be flown into a temporary camp at the work site. Capital investment in a town site would be much lower (no schools, no need for recreation or any permanent facilities), and when the resource is played out, the camp would simply be dismantled and removed. Whatever the social benefits of such an arrangement for the workers might be, it means that even fewer of the benefits of resource development would remain in the North or at least in the larger communities in the region, and an even greater percentage of the financial returns will flow to the south.

The fly-in camp, which may well be the most economically rational approach to northern resource development, and certainly gives corporations and developers more freedom to act, is really a contemporary and in some ways a starker version of the old colonial process. The idea makes it even more obvious than in the past that northern resources belong first to the corporation that develops them, and secondly to the nation, and that there will be little return, and none of a permanent nature, to the regions that are their source. When a temporary camp closes, all that will be left is a scar on the environment — a minor one if proper precautions are taken — and little else.

Native people, as has been made clear, do not share this southern vision of the North's future. Unlike the developers, they trace their ancestry back in the region for centuries, and typically have no wish to live elsewhere. Their priorities are naturally therefore different from those of newcomers from the south. These priorities are not monolithic; some Native groups are opposed to resource development, while others are willing to participate in it so long as they are assured a share of whatever benefits it brings, and so long as the environment is not seriously affected by it. But one thing Native groups across the Provincial Norths have in common when under pressure from development is that, until very recently, they have lacked the financial and political resources to deal with it.

Much of the northern reaches of the provinces — northern Alberta, Saskatchewan, Manitoba, and Ontario — is covered by old treaties, signed in the nineteenth and early twentieth centuries, when Native people were by law second-class citizens and the region was frankly viewed as a frigid wasteland where no non-Native in his right mind would live any longer than it took to extract whatever wealth could be found there. The treaties provided a small range of benefits in return for the extinguishment of aboriginal title to enormous tracts of land. But through carelessness or neglect, even these benefits were denied to some Native groups who should have received them — the case of the Lubicon Cree is the most notorious. In the regions not covered by treaty — northern British Columbia, Labrador, and parts of northern Quebec — the Native people were denied even what benefits the security of formally established reserves could provide. The silver lining in this cloud, at least for those who are not currently under treaty, is that the treaties now being negotiated are vastly more generous than the old ones.

It is easy to understand the increasing level of frustration of the indigenous people of the Provincial Norths, even for those who may not be particularly sympathetic towards it. For, despite all the talk of indigenous self-government and bringing Native people within the framework of the Canadian constitution, the reality is that these people have very little control over the activities that threaten the foundations of their lives.

It was this feeling of powerlessness, combined with a sense of impending loss (as well as a newly-developed awareness of the techniques by which such issues are brought before the public) that led the Innu to march on a NATO airbase to protest low-level fighter flights over their hunting grounds, and which convinced the Lubicon Cree of the need to set up blockades to stop oil development on the lands they claimed. It was for similar reasons that the Gitskan-We'etseweten spent millions of dollars and several years of effort in an ultimately unsuccessful appeal to the British Columbia Supreme Court for recognition of their land claim. The clashes are becoming more emotional, with threats to shoot down helicopters in the James Bay region, tense standoffs in Gitskan territory between Natives and loggers, similar episodes in northern Ontario, and Cree hunters angry over Manitoba Hydro's plans to build new dams on their land.

There is evidence that these tactics are having the desired result, for the Innu, the Lubicon Cree, the Gitskan, and the James Bay Cree have all found considerable support for their cause, both from indigenous people and from non-Native sympathizers within and without the Provincial Norths. In British Columbia, the United Church of Canada gave $1 million for aboriginal land claims in a sign of solidarity with indigenous aspirations. The James Bay Cree and the Inuit to the north of them have achieved a remarkable degree of success in winning allies among environmentally-sensitive residents of the northeastern United States, and have actually managed to delay (if not derail) Phase II of the huge James Bay project, especially through the cancellation in 1992 of American contracts for its power — a few thousand Cree and their allies standing in front of a billion dollar juggernaut. The New Democratic Party government in Ontario moved quickly after its election in 1990 to deal with several difficult aboriginal issues in the province's North, including the potentially violent situation in the Temagami forest. The election of the NDP in British Columbia in the fall of 1991 was soon followed by an announcement that the government would recognize aboriginal land rights and expedite the land claims process, thus raising the possibility that a century of Native demands for a treaty would be fulfilled. There are still many issues to be settled, some of them seemingly intractable, but these well-publicized breakthroughs suggest that the juggernaut of development without consultation and consent may have been slowed down, if not stopped.

Although the Provincial Norths have not yet spoken with a united voice, choruses of complaint have from time to time arisen in the Norths of individual provinces, and in at least one case the complaints have coalesced into a serious, or semi-serious northern separatist movement. There had been sporadic talk of secession in northern Ontario as early as 1891, and in 1906 a petition requesting the establishment of a new province of Algoma was forwarded to the Laurier government. A few years later some residents of Sudbury proposed a new province of Huronia; in the post–World War II years Hubert Limbrick, a city councillor from Fort William (now part of Thunder Bay) agitated for the province of Aurora, so named because it heralded "The Golden Dawn of a New Day." All of these movements were based on dissatisfaction with the alleged mistreatment of the North and its people by the provincial government. Some were based on quite specific complaints: Huronia was a reaction to grievances over provincial mining legislation. The Toronto *Globe* expressed the dismissive reaction of those who controlled the province: "Unfortunately, such talk is not merely ridiculous," it sniffed in 1906, "it does harm by keeping up a feeling of unrest in the minds of those who are unaquainted with the character of the obstacles that make such a scheme utterly impracticable."

The most sustained campaign for a new province, this time to be called "New Ontario," was headed by Ed Deibel, a motel owner and civic booster from North Bay (a "northern" community only 200 km north of Toronto) who in 1977 collected 10,000 signatures on a petition, enough to register his Northern Ontario Heritage Party as an official party within the province. Like its predecessors, this party focused on a small range of strongly felt grievances. An early one, for instance, was the provincial sales tax on fuel and energy, which was felt to be unfair because of the distances and climate of the North. Deibel sent a list of ten demands to Premier Davis, with a promise that if the government accepted them he would abandon his campaign for a new province. Davis replied with reasoned arguments and soothing words. The demand that perhaps spoke most urgently to a problem common to all Provincial Norths was "at least 50 per cent of all natural resources to be processed and manufactured in Northern Ontario." To this Davis replied "My government is actively engaged in negotiation ... to fund development strategies ... we anticipate substantial growth ... Arbitrary limits such as the 50 percent you suggest are often more confining than a flexible policy for stimulating growth."

The Northern Ontario Heritage Party had some difficulty in deciding whether it really wanted a new province, and Deibel bridled at the suggestion that he was a separatist: "If Northerners are forced to create a new province we will be like all the other provinces," he stated. "We won't be separate or different from anyone else ... We're 100 per cent Canadians. Secessionist maybe; but separatists, no." But inevitably, after a year or so of discussion, the idea of a separate northern province faded, victim of indifference, adherence to the status quo, and the failure of its supporters to articulate anything more than a list of regional grievances against the provincial government.

Southern support for many issues vital to the Provincial Norths has originated, at least in part, in the contemporary environmental movement. The marriage of indigenous and environmental issues has not always been a happy or successful one, as witness the role of the Greenpeace movement in the European boycott of the products of the Canadian fur trade, which had a detrimental effect on the Native people of the North who still depended on returns from hunting and trapping. On other matters, however, there was greater co-operation. In the debates raging in British Columbia over logging, in Ontario over the future of that province's northern forests, in Quebec over the grand designs of Hydro-Québec, the Native people and environmentalists often found themselves on the same side of the issues. There is some irony in the sight of southerners, some of whom have never been to the North, rallying to the defence of the northern environment, but the net effect has been to increase the power and the influence of indigenous protesters and to provide a southern base of support for their activities.

The environmental movement, as it deals with the Provincial Norths, contains a certain element of sentiment and nostalgia. Southerners, often living in degraded urban environments which are able to survive partly by the importation of power and resources from the North, seek to preserve the remains of pristine wilderness which they have perhaps never visited. This means in effect that they are anxious to impose standards of environmental purity on regions that they have never seen which are more stringent than those they would apply to their own surroundings. Whatever the motives, however, the result is that environmental protection has emerged as a major element in the development of the Provincial Norths. It is not always the decisive element, as the history of dams in northern Manitoba and the first phase of the James Bay project shows, but it can carry great weight, and some major plans have been delayed or scotched by the alliance of Native and environmentalist organizations. Plans for a huge pulp and paper development in northern Alberta have been blocked by concerns about the future of the Mackenzie River drainage basin, just as the proposed Hydro-Québec plans for the second stage of the James Bay project have come under an effective attack by environmentalists and the James Bay Cree.

One problem with these coalitions formed between indigenous northerners (and non-indigenous northern sympathizers too, for there is a sizeable group of them in the region as well) and southern environmentalists is that it can impose a certain model on the North which may be even more rigid than the old one, and which may not be appropriate to the region. The current battle over the killing of fur-bearing animals is a case in point. Both the old system, in which indigenous people were encouraged to kill animals freely, and the new environmentalist position, which views the killing of a single animal for profit as an abomination, are equally heedless of what the Native people themselves may want, and in this respect Greenpeace is worse than the Hudson's Bay Company. It is quite clear that Native people are not adamantly or uniformly opposed on principle to development or logging, mining, and other resource projects per se. What they do oppose is the model of development in which they have virtually no power over what takes place, and receive very few of the benefits of the economic activity.

It has often been observed that all Canadians have much to learn from the First Nations people, particularly as regards indigenous spirituality, their attitude towards the natural world, and their oral traditions. But there is a lesson to be learned specifically from those First Nations people who live in the Provincial Norths. The lesson arises from their continuing efforts to secure a share of the benefits arising from the economic development of their homelands. First Nations people place less emphasis than southern developers on the market-sensitive exploitation of commercial opportunities. The traditional southern-based development has followed a cycle of boom and bust, transferring wealth from the region, and leaving nothing behind but damage when it is gone. Indigenous inhabitants, who are permanent residents of the region, wish to ensure stability and prosperity for themselves and their children, and thus come to the question of resource development from quite a different perspective. For them, resources are to be developed as the people who own them — the Native community — require, and according to a schedule which maximizes returns to the community rather than quick profits for investors. This means that the priority is on the development of resources over time, or, if development must occur quickly, then sufficient money must be put aside to provide for the time when development is finished. This might be done through royalty payments which could be reinvested in the community (as in the northern comprehensive land claims), or in some other manner which ensures long-term benefits to the people. An example of the difference in attitudes is what happened when oil revenues were paid to the Native people of northern British Columbia some years ago. When, after long delays and court proceedings, the money was at last paid, a number of sharp operators from the south loaded stereos, televisions, cars, and luxury goods onto trucks and took them to the communities, expecting the money to burn a hole in the Natives' pockets and fall into their hands. To their chagrin, the community members took their royalties to the bank and put them in medium-term deposits. Much of the money was subsequently used to finance band-constructed housing.

Though such incidents are welcome object lessons in an age of crass materialism, and certainly break old stereotypes about indigenous peoples' attitude to money, the real message from the Native people of the Provincial Norths is one that applies more generally than simply a welcome alternative to the poverty and instability of indigenous communities. Their development model is one that holds the prospect of breaking the colonial cycle that currently persists in the North, at least insofar as it concerns economic development. Certainly the idea of royalties paid to an indigenous community and used for long rather than short-term purposes has an application which is wider than just northern Native communities.

For the Provincial Norths to break the colonial pattern of development and resource exploitation, therefore, a new economic model is required. It need not be hostile to capital-ism, nor to investment, since the issue is one of priorities and approach, not ideology. The model is one that concentrates on the careful and sustained exploitation or development of re-sources, with a view to the protection of the environment and the economic and social long-term future. One example of such an indigenous approach to an economic venture is the James Bay Cree's operation of Air Creebec, a commercial ven-ture which gives priority to serving local needs rather than maximizing returns for investors. There is no reason why such an approach should not benefit all northerners, both non-Na-tive and indigenous, as well as provide the region with a new level of stability.

Unfortunately, the Air Creebec model does not seem likely to spawn many imitators. The reason for pessimism lies in the fact that gains of this sort tend to be made after the fact. The James Bay Cree, for example, have been fighting for nearly twenty years now to force the government of Quebec to honour all aspects of the accord which enabled them to pur-chase the airline. To put it another way, the gains for the Cree that brought their airline into being were not part of any government policy of generosity or a thought-out plan, but the fruits of a long struggle waged in the courts and in the forum of public opinion. Similarly, the Lubicon Cree are nearing an agreement with the federal and provincial governments, but only after their land and hunting grounds have been harmed and their way of life seriously disrupted. Our country does well with guilt, reparations for past wrongs, and compensation of various kinds, but such post hoc reparations do not constitute planning. Nevertheless, the Native leaders and elders possess remarkable patience, and have almost always rejected the option of violence and confrontation, raising the possibility that eventually their approach to the future of their land may be taken more seriously by the rest of the country.

Perhaps the greatest barrier to a new future for the Provincial Norths is the lack of a common identity. Although the region shares a great deal — its climate, geography, racial mixture, economic past, the attitude of federal and provincial governments towards it, often fanciful and unrealistic national dreams of its economic potential — there is nothing in this country even approaching a regional identity for the Provincial Norths, nor a sense of shared destiny. In a few places, such as the Peace River country of northern Alberta and British Columbia, and in Labrador, there is certainly a local sense of identity, but there is nothing that spans the nation, no effort to address mutual problems.

There have been some small but promising initiatives that have brought people from the Provincial Norths together. The Arctic Winter Games, for example, which were originally designed for the Territorial Norths and international partners, has admitted representatives of the Provincial Norths as well. More significantly, associations committed to the preservation of single-industry towns have brought together people from across the country, many of them from the Provincial Norths. But the question tends to be discussed as a shared economic problem, not as a problem with a regional focus. And, partly because of the other strains on the Canadian nation, such associations do not really generate a sense of regional experience. The aspirations of Nouveau Québec, for instance, do not fit easily into anglophone plans for the Provincial Norths, nor have many attempts been made to bring together Native and non-Native residents of the region to address shared concerns.

The future of the Provincial Norths remain uncertain — this is true enough for all of Canada in the 1990s, but pertains in a particular way to this neglected region. There is no question that its resources hold tremendous significance for all Canadians, who cast covetous eyes on northern hydro-electric potential, mineral deposits, timber resources, and hydro-carbon reserves; their vision of northern development is one that demands that these resources be extracted according to the needs and interests of those living outside the region, and increasingly, of those living outside Canada. The realities of population distribution, political power, and capitalism do not hold out a bright promise for an improvement in regional conditions. At the same time, there does not seem to be much prospect of a new rapprochement between Native and non-Native residents of the Provincial Norths. Resource development that is opposed to the patterns and rhythms of the indigenous economy means that battle lines have in places been drawn between racial groups in the region. As many Native people report, and as others can attest, racial tensions are nowhere more acute than in northern resource towns. The well-deserved (but improving) reputation of Kenora, Ontario is a case in point, as is the episode of Kitty Osborne's murder in The Pas, Manitoba, an infamous scandal brought to public attention recently through the book and television program *Conspiracy of Silence*. Aboriginal land claims in British Columbia often take the shape of a contest between the futures of the Native and non-Native communities, and thus generate much tension and uncertainty, though there are always exceptions. There are also a significant number of non-Native northerners who support aboriginal land claims and share the claimants' vision of the future. But it is unlikely that a majority of northerners will soon come to share this point of view.

Nor is it likely that many federal and provincial politicians will soon come to the defence of the Provincial Norths, for there are comparatively few votes in the region. No politician, not even one from the North, has formed a cohesive vision of it as a region, or sought to build lines of connection with similar regions across the country; mostly they have asked, like Oliver Twist, and often with the same lack of success, simply for "more." The Yukon and the Northwest Territories seem to have cornered the market on southerners' interest in and sympathy for the North and its people, its beauty, history, and romance. The prospect of empowering the vast region of the Provincial Norths, rich in resources but thinly populated, rarely emerges in national or provincial discourse, though it is a constant topic of concern in the regions themselves. During the debate about the future of Quebec, to take a current example, it became apparent that Québécois, whether federalist or separatist, view the North of the province as a resource treasure chest, and that it has never occurred to them that the region might have a view of the future which differs from theirs, or a different economic agenda.

It would be foolhardy to try to predict the future of the Provincial Norths — whether they will continue to follow the path of powerlessness and political impotence, aboriginal dislocation and despair, and non-Native transiency that has marked them until now, or whether they will experience a new empowerment. There are few signs of a real change in national attitudes, or even much evidence that the new environmentalism will have lasting success. Have the James Bay Cree and their allies really halted the expansion of the massive hydro projects, or only delayed them? Have the pulp and paper projects planned for northern Alberta been scuttled? Will the aboriginal and environmentalist protest over the construction of the Kemano Dam in northern British Columbia succeed, or will Alcan win its appeal and proceed with the project? All these issues could be resolved either way. The American philosopher George Santayana said that those who do not know their history are condemned to repeat it, and given the painful history of mega-projects in the Provincial Norths to date it is distressing to observe how little has been learned from them.

As individual regions, the Provincial Norths have little chance of making their influence felt within the nation. Many of their battles, fought singly, are subsumed into the arena of provincial politics. It takes a project and a protest on the scale of the Great Whale River episode, or an act of racial colonialism on the order of the handling of the Lubicon Cree case to make an issue a national one. And even then, such issues are seen as development issues or racial ones, and not as northern issues, rooted in a centuries-old pattern of internal colonialism. Until the Provincial Norths are seen as a single region, with distinct but shared economic, social, cultural, and environmental concerns, there is little chance of improvement in the situation. Without a strong regional voice the fragmentation of the Provincial Norths will continue, weakening their one possible source of empowerment. A step in the right direction was the establishment of the Interprovincial Conference of Ministries Responsible for Northern Development, which met for the first time at Fort McMurray in 1978 for the purpose of exchanging information and ideas. The Conference, which meets annually, serves notice of the growing awareness of the importance of the Provincial Norths.

Developing a regional identity will not be easy, however, for the distances involved are vast and the cultures, despite their shared problems, varied. Imagine a journey from Atlin, British Columbia to Nain or Hebron in Labrador, a distance of about 7,000 km in a straight line (if the journey could be done in a straight line, which it cannot), and four time zones (four and a half if the journey continues to northern Newfoundland). Think of the welter of cultures in the region, the different aboriginal groups with different languages, customs, and cultures; agricultural settlements in northern British Columbia, Alberta, and Ontario, brand-new company towns like Tumbler Ridge, British Columbia, old company towns like Rouyn, Quebec, decaying company towns like Elliot Lake, Ontario, and Schefferville, Quebec, company ghost towns like Uranium City, Saskatchewan, well-established, diversified communities like Thompson and The Pas, Manitoba, isolated Native communities from Shamattawa to Sheshatshit, some of them stable, some infected with social pathologies. Add to this a mixture of ideological differences, from pro-development to hard-core environmentalists, from Native leaders to representatives of the mainstream political parties, and one gains some sense of the difficulty of building a coherent identity in the Provincial Norths. But perhaps the alternative — a continuation of the past — would be worse, certainly for the region, and perhaps for the nation as well.

If the residents of the Provincial Norths could realize the commonality of their situation and the fact that they could be allied against similar external forces, they could find the seeds of a common future. Individually they have little power, but together they could have strength, at least enough to demand a national hearing. Even a consortium of their members of Parliament, though it would never form a powerful block, would number twenty or more, and such a voice, if united, could not be ignored.

Perhaps most important is the fact that even the most preliminary discussions across the Provincial Norths would raise the consideration of its concerns out of the morass of local squabbles — over corporate plans, individual aboriginal land claims, demands for more largesse from provincial governments — to a different plane, where debate would focus on the systemic and national problems facing the region as a whole. Once discussion reached this level, it is possible that the Provincial *North*, as a region rather than the Provincial *Norths*, a series of regions, would be able to develop a consensus on issues, or at least recognize that it has a tremendous amount in common. Political visionaries might dream of redrafting provincial boundaries to take the common interests of the northern districts into account; the very nature of internal colonization makes such a thing unlikely, but to speak the dream would raise the consciousness of the region, and as the recent history of Europe, Asia, and if we are unlucky, Quebec has shown, national boundaries are not carved in stone.

The Provincial North, seen as a whole, is a vast and varied land, ranging from the rocky shores of Labrador to the barren lands of Nouveau Québec and the heavily forested hills of northern British Columbia. It contains vast economic resources, some still undiscovered, many not exploited. It also has rich human resources, yet for all its potential, it is a troubled land. Aboriginal villages have witnessed the virtual collapse of their culture and language, have seen their traditional economies damaged or destroyed, and now struggle with seemingly intractable social problems. Non-Native communities in the region have not been spared social problems, and are marked by high levels of transiency, and economic uncertainty.

Residents of the Provincial Norths have not accepted these conditions passively. Native leaders and organizations have brought their causes to public attention by a variety of means, some quite confrontational. Others have worked more quietly within their communities to preserve their language, enhance the role of the elders, and to ensure that their traditions and customs are passed on to a younger generations. Still others are working in anti-alcohol and anti-drug programs, or are seeking to increase their control of the education system. Non-Natives are similarly trying to solve the social and economic problems in northern communities, especially to secure and broaden their economic base, to make sure that their children and grandchildren will be able to stay and make a living in the region.

But economic logic works against many of these efforts to build a new Provincial North. Fly-in mining camps will not contribute much to the long-term viability of the region. It is still often cheaper to remove the resources to southern processing plants, thus ensuring that most of the jobs and benefits from these resources will continue to flow southward, or increasingly, out of the country. Colonialism works on the assumption that wealth flows towards the centre, and power out from it; this has been the structure of the Provincial Norths since the early days of the fur trade, and will remain so until the region is able to secure a greater share of its resource revenues, and to find a unified voice in the corridors of power.

While the responsibility for the creation of a new North across Canada's sub-Arctic fringe must rest with the region, it is at the same time necessary for all Canadians to adopt a new perspective on the region. It is important for the country to recognize the degree to which Canadian prosperity is based on the massive transfer of resources and wealth out of the Provincial Norths. The region is not a poor relation of Confederation, begging for handouts; it is rich, but it is powerless. Imagine, if possible, a Canada without the hydro-electric power, the forest, mineral, and other resources that come from the Provincial Norths. What the region needs is not charity, but an equitable re-distribution, in the form of permanent jobs, resource revenues, and political power, of the wealth that it produces.

As the end of the century approaches, the Provincial Norths are lands of divided dreams: developers with visions of resource wealth, of provincial politicians hoping to maintain vast internal empires, of non-Native workers looking for prosperity in short-term jobs in a land that will never become home. It is a land of Native leaders who are struggling for a better life for their people, and of environmentalists who see the region as a battleground for the preservation of pristine wilderness. Some of these visions are incompatible, and reconciling them will not be easy, particularly since the region lacks a sense of common identity and a shared future.

The boundaries of the Provincial Norths, though created by politicians who knew little about the regions they were separating, are artificial yet powerful lines. They divide a vast region into provincial fiefdoms where lines of communication, power, and wealth run north-south rather than across it. The task for the next decade is for the region to challenge the past, and to bring together the divided dreams and perspectives that have fragmented discussions of its history and its future. This is the challenge of the Provincial Norths, the opportunity to create a new North, to wrestle, as the Territorial North has done, with the political and economic bonds of colonialism, and to gain a new control over the future. The task will be difficult, for the forces ranged against it are powerful. But within the effort may rest a re-evaluation of the foundations of Canada's attitude towards the North, towards resource development, and towards to role of Native people within Confederation. This surely makes the barriers to the creation of a common identity worth testing, and should sustain and inspire those willing to work towards the creation of a new identity in the Provincial Norths.

Suggested Readings

Although there exists no previous general history of the Provincial Norths, there are a few books which include an extensive treatment of the region as part of a larger survey of the entire North. Chief among them are two volumes by Morris Zaslow, which are essential sources of material on the region: *The Opening of the Canadian North, 1870–1914* (Toronto: McClelland and Stewart, 1967) and *The Northward Expansion of Canada, 1914–1967* (Toronto: McClelland and Stewart, 1988). Also invaluable is Robert Bone's *The Geography of the Canadian North* (Toronto: Oxford University Press, 1992). Probably the most useful bibliographical tool is yet to be published; the forthcoming volume edited by the present authors, *The Historiography of the Provincial Norths*, is intended to serve as an extensive guide to the literature on the individual provinces.

The main difficulty with suggesting sources for the study of the history of the northern parts of the provinces is that the best academic histories of the provinces generally treat their norths in a perfunctory way or not at all. Those books which do deal with the subject, on the other hand, tend to be chronicles written by enthusiasts, which though often engrossing, are not always reliable and almost never analytical. This is by and large true of all the provinces covered in this book. Probably the best works on the early Provincial Norths are those that deal with the fur trade period, such as E. E. Rich's *The Fur Trade and the Northwest to 1857* (Toronto: McClelland and Stewart, 1967), and the other numerous works published by the Hudson's Bay Record Society, although these of course deal with only one period of the region's history. It goes without saying that any serious research into the topic must begin with the finding aids in the archives of the individual provinces.

Nevertheless, there is a wealth of material on the subject, and some valuable scholarly studies in the periodical literature. The student of British Columbia's Provincial North should consult Father Adrien Morice, *History of the Northern Interior of British Columbia, (formerly New Caledonia)* (London: John Lane, 1906; reprinted 1978); Robin Fisher, *Contact and Conflict: Indian-European Relations in British Columbia, 1774–1890* (Vancouver: University of British Columbia Press, 1977); Jean Barman, *The West Beyond the West: A History of British Columbia* (Toronto: University of Toronto Press, 1991); G. E. Bowes, ed., *Peace River Chronicles* (Vancouver: Prescott, 1963); K. S. Coates and W. R. Morrison, *The Alaska Highway in World War II: The U.S. Army of Occupation in Canada's Northwest* (Norman, OK: University of Oklahoma Press, 1992); W. Duff, *The Indian History of British Columbia*, Vol. I (Victoria: B.C. Provincial Museum, 1965); K. R. Fladmark, "Early Fur-trade Forts of the Peace River Area of British Columbia," *BC Studies* 65 (1985), 48-65; H. and K. T. McCullum, *Caledonia: 100 Years Ahead* (Toronto: Anglican Book Centre,

1979); T. Thorner, ed., *Sa Ts'e: Historical Perspectives on Northern British Columbia* (Prince George: College of New Caledonia, 1989); R. Ridington, *Trail to Heaven: Knowledge and Narrative in a Northern Native Community* (Vancouver: Douglas and McIntyre, 1988).

For Alberta, see René Fumoleau, *As Long as This Land Shall Last: A History of Treaties 8 and 11* (Toronto: McClelland and Stewart, 1973); James G. MacGregor, *A History of Alberta* (Edmonton: Hurtig, 1972); E. E. Hoskin, ed., *"I Remember" Peace River, Alberta and Adjacent Districts, 1914–1916,* Part II (Peace River: The Woman's Institute of Peace River, 1976); R. E. English, "An Economic History of Northern Alberta," Ph.D. thesis, University of Toronto, n.d.; Dene Wodih Society, *Wolverine Myths and Visions: Dene Traditions from Northern Alberta* (Edmonton: University of Alberta, 1990); P. Driben, *We Are Metis: The Ethnography of a Halfbreed Community in Northern Alberta* (New York: AMS Press, 1985); Alberta, Northern Development Group, *The Economy of Northern Alberta: Bibliography* (Edmonton, 1975); R. C. Daniel, "Indian Rights and Hinterland Resources: The Case of Northern Alberta", MA thesis, University of Alberta, 1977; Co-West Associates, *A Social and Economic Overview of Northern Alberta* (Edmonton: Northern Alberta Development Council, 1981); Northern Development Branch, *Summary of Social and Economic Circumstances, Northern Alberta* (Edmonton: Business Development and Tourism, 1977); E. Schneider, *Ribbons of Steel: The Story of the Northern Alberta Railways* (Calgary: Detselig Enterprises, 1989); J. J. Fitzgerald, *Black Gold with Grit: The Alberta Oil Sands* (Sidney, B.C.: Gray's Publishing, 1978); D. J. Comfort, *The Abscand Fiasco: The Rise and Fall of a Brave Oil Sands Extraction Plant* (Edmonton: Freisen Printers, 1980).

Saskatchewan's historiography has naturally concentrated on its southern agricultural regions. But A. S. Morton, the province's first great historian, did devote a substantial portion of his massive *A History of the Canadian West,* 2nd ed. (Toronto: University of Toronto Press, 1979) to the fur trade in the northern Prairie provinces. Also invaluable is E. E. Rich and A. M. Johnson, eds., *Cumberland House Journals and Inland Journals, 1775–1782,* First and Second Series (London: Hudson's Bay Record Society, 14 and 15, 1951 and 1952). See also D. Meyer, "The Prehistory of Northern Saskatchewan" in H. T. Epp and I. Dyck, *Tracking Ancient Hunters: Prehistoric Archaeology in Saskatchewan* (Regina: Saskatchewan Archaeological Society, 1983); R. Jarvenpa and H. J. Brombach, "The Microeconomics of Southern Chipewyan Fur Trade History," in S. Krech III, ed., *The Subarctic Fur Trade* (Vancouver: University of British Columbia Press, 1984); J. S. H. Brown and R. Brightman, eds., *"The Orders of the Dreamed:" George Nelson on Cree and Northern Ojibwa Religion and Myth, 1823* (Winnipeg: University of Manitoba Press, 1988); H. M. S. Kemp, *Northern Trader* (London: Jarrolds, 1957); S. A. Keighley, *Trader-Tripper-Trapper: The Life of a Bay Man* (Winnipeg: Watson and Dwyer, 1989); W. F. Payton, *An Historical Sketch of the Diocese of Saskatchewan of the Anglican Church of Canada* (n.p., 1974); B. Benoit, "The Mission at Ile a la Crosse," in *The Beaver,* Winter 1980; G. Abrams, *Prince Albert: The First Century, 1866–1966* (Saskatoon: Modern Press, 1966); J. B. Waldram, *As Long as the Rivers Run: Hydroelectric Development and Native Communities in Western Canada* (Winnipeg: University of Manitoba Press, 1988); M. Dobbin, *The One-And-A-Half Men: The Story of Jim Brady and Malcolm Morris, Metis Patriots of the Twentieth Century* (Vancouver: New Star Books, 1981); J. Harding, *Aboriginal*

Rights and Government Wrongs: Uranium Mining and NeoColonialism in Northern Saskatchewan (Regina: University of Regina, 1988).

The student looking for sources on the history of northern Manitoba should consult the following: Richard Ens, *A Bibliography of Northern Manitoba* (Winnipeg: University of Manitoba Press, 1991); D. J. Teillet, *A Northern Manitoba Bibliography* (Ottawa: Department of Regional Economic Expansion, 1979); W. L. Morton, *Northern Manitoba* (Winnipeg: Government of Manitoba, 1950); G. Dickson, *Prehistoric Northern Manitoba* (Winnipeg: Manitoba Museum of Man and Nature, 1977); A. J. Ray, *Indians in the Fur Trade* (Toronto: University of Toronto Press, 1974); Howard Fleming, *Canada's Arctic Outlet: A History of the Hudson's Bay Company* (Berkeley: University of California Press, 1957); P. D. Elias, *Metropolis and Hinterland in Northern Manitoba* (Winnipeg: Manitoba Museum of Man and Nature, 1975); G. Malaher, *The North I Love* (Winnipeg: Hyperion Press, 1984); R. Robson, "Flin Flon: A Study of Company-Community Relations in a Single Enterprise Community," *Urban History*, Vol. 12, February 1984; R. Robson, "Manitoba's Resource Towns: The Twentieth Century Frontier," *Labour/Le Travailleur*, Vol. 12 (Autumn, 1983).

Like the other provinces, Ontario lacks a comprehensive scholarly history of its northern region. A popular approach to the subject is M. Bray and E. Epp, eds., *A Vast and Magnificent Land: An Illustrated History of Northern Ontario* (Sudbury and Thunder Bay: Laurentian and Lakehead Universities, 1984), but the region's history must be gleaned from more local and specialized works. Useful works are K. C. A. Dawson, *Prehistory of Northern Ontario* (Thunder Bay: Thunder Bay Historical Museum Society, 1983); J. G. Kohl, *Kitchi-Gami: Life Among the Lake Superior Ojibway* (St. Paul, MN: Minnesota Historical Society Press, 1985); V. P. Lytwyn, *The Fur Trade of the Little North: Indians, Pedlars, and Englishmen East of Lake Winnipeg, 1760–1821* (Winnipeg: Rupert's Land Research Centre, University of Winnipeg, 1986); M. Zaslow, "The Dilemmas of the Northern Missionary Diocese: The Case of the Anglican See of Moosonee," *Lakehead University Review/Revue de l'Université laurentienne* 11, no. 2; D. Newell, *Technology on the Frontier: Mining in Old Ontario* (Vancouver: University of British Columbia Press, 1986); P. Smith, *Harvest From the Rock: A History of Mining in Ontario* (Toronto: Macmillan, 1986); E. Arthur, ed., *The Thunder Bay District, 1821–1892* (Toronto: University of Toronto Press, 1973); A. Tucker, *Steam Into Wilderness* (Toronto: Fitzhenry and Whiteside, 1978); O. S. Nock, *Algoma and Central Railway* (London: Adam & Charles Black, 1975); H. V. Nelles, *The Politics of Development: Forests, Mines and Hydro-Electric Power in Ontario, 1849–1941* (Toronto: Macmillan, 1974); R. S. Lambert and P. Pross, *Renewing Nature's Wealth: A Centennial History of the Public Management of Lands, Forests, and Wildlife in Ontario, 1763–1967* (n.p.: Ontario Department of Land and Forests, 1967); I. Radforth, *Bushworkers and Bosses: Logging in Northern Ontario, 1900–1980* (Toronto: University of Toronto Press, 1987); B. W. Hodgins and J. Benedickson, *The Temagami Experience: Recreation, Resources, and Aboriginal Rights in the Northern Ontario Wilderness* (Toronto: University of Toronto Press, 1989); M. Zaslow, "Does Northern Ontario Possess a Regional Identity?" *Lakehead University Review/Revue de l'Université laurentienne* 5, no. 4; G. Weller, "Hinterland Politics: The Case of Northern Ontario," *Canadian Journal of Political Science*, 10, no. 4.

Quebec has a substantial literature in both official languages, much of it recently on the James Bay project. A good introduction to the subject may be found in D. Francis and T. Morantz, *Partners in Fur: A History of the Fur Trade in Eastern James Bay, 1600–1870* (Kingston and Montreal: McGill-Queen's University Press, 1983); E. S. Rogers, *The Quest for Food and Furs: The Mistassini Cree, 1953–54* (Ottawa: National Museum of Man, 1973); F. G. Speck, *Naskapi: The Savage Hunters of the Labrador Peninsula* (Ottawa: National Museum of Man, 1973); A. P. Low, *Report on Explorations in James' Bay and Country East of Hudson Bay, Drained by Big, Great Whale and Clearwater River* (Montreal: W. F. Brown, 1888); Québec, *Colonisation, Mines, et Pecheries: Extraits de rapports sur le district d'Ungava recemment annexé à la province de Québec et constituent le Nouveau Québec* (Quebec: E. E. Cinq-Mars, 1929); T. R. Moore, ed., *Future Directions for Research in Nouveau Québec* (Montreal: Centre for Northern Studies and Research, McGill University, 1984); "La colonisation du Nouveau Québec," Societé de Géographie de Québec, *Bulletin* 20, 4-5 (juil.-dec. 1926); M. Brochu, *Le Defi du Nouveau-Québec: la question equimaude, la situation economique, presence necessaire de Québec* (Montreal: Editions du Jour, 1962); N. Rouland, *Les Inuit du Nouveau-Québec et la Convention de la Baie James* (Quebec: Association Inuksiutiit Katimajiit et Centre d'Etudes Nordiques, Université Laval, 1978); R. MacGregor, *Chief: The Fearless Vision of Billy Diamond* (Markham, Ont.: Viking, 1989); S. Vincent, and G. Bowers, eds., *Baie James et Nord Québecois: Dix An Après* (Montreal: Recherches Amerindiennes au Québec, 1988); I. E. LaRusic, *Negotiating a Way of Life: Initial Cree Experience with the Administrative Structure Arising from the James Bay Agreement* (Ottawa: Department of Indian Affairs and Northern Development, 1979);

Perhaps because Labrador is geographically separate from the rest of Newfoundland, there are several books that deal specifically with it as a distinct region. But most general histories of the province — the first two volumes of J. R. Smallwood's *The Book of Newfoundland* (St. John's: Newfoundland Book Publishers, 1937), for instance, include little material on Labrador. Useful sources are A. Cooke and F. Caron, Bibliography of the Quebec-Labrador Peninsula (Boston: G. K. Hall, 1968); R. Budgell, *A Survey of Labrador Material in Newfoundland and Labrador Archives* (Goose Bay: Labrador Institute of Northern Studies, 1985); W. G. Gosling's *Labrador* (London: A. Rivers, 1910); J. Tuck, *Newfoundland and Labrador Prehistory* (Ottawa: National Museum of Man,1976); G. Cartwright, *Journal of Transactions and Events, During a Residence of Seventeen Years on the Coast of Labrador* (Newark [U.K.]: Allin and Ridge, 3 vols., 1792); H.Y. Hind, *Explorations in the Interior of the Labrador Peninsula* (London: Longman, Roberts & Green, 1863); G. Henriksen, *Hunters in the Barrens* (St. John's: Institute of Social and Economic Research, Memorial University, 1973); P. Armitage, *The Innu* (The Naskapi-Montagnais) (New York: Chelsea House, 1991); M. Wadden, *Nitassin* (Vancouver: Douglas and McIntyre, 1991); H. A. Innis, *The Cod Fisheries: The History of an International Economy* (Toronto: University of Toronto Press, 1978); *Periodical Accounts* (Moravian Mission Board, 1790-1970); F. W. Peacock, *Reflections From a Snowhouse* (St. John's: Jesperson Press, 1986); N. Smith, *Fifty-Two Years at the Labrador Fishery* (London: A. H. Stockwell, 1936); R. Geren and B. McCullogh, *Cain's Legacy: The Building of the Iron Ore Company of Canada* (Sept-Iles: Iron Ore Company of Canada, 1990); P. Smith, *Brinco: The Story of Churchill Falls* (Toronto: McClelland and Stewart, 1975); M. B. Loder, *Daughter of Labrador* (St. John's: H. Cuff, 1989); R. Rompkey, *Grenfell of Labrador* (Toronto: University of Toronto Press, 1991).

Index

Abitibi, 56
Agricultural settlement, 54-57
Agriculture, commercial, 6, 13, 57
Air Creebec, 108, 124
Air links, 90
Alaska Highway, 42, 63, 64
Albany River, 15, 36
Alberta, 38, 40, 51, 97
Alberta district, 36
Alberta-Pacific Forest Products,
    100
Alcan, 115
Alcohol, 27, 77, 107
Algoma, 120
Andras, Robert, 3
Anglican Church, 80
Anik satellite, 90
Arctic Winter Games, 125
Assiniboia district, 37
Athabasca district, 27, 36
Athabasca tar sands, 53
Atiwapiskat River, 15
Atlantic Ocean, 13

Barkerville, 47
Basque, 23
Beattie Gold mines, 49
Beaufort Sea, 12
Bennett, W. A. C., 43-44, 91, 101
Berens River, 82
Bombardier, J. A., 90
Bone, Robert, 6
Borden, Robert, 40
Boundary disputes,
    Newfoundland and Quebec, 35
    Ontario and Manitoba, 36
    Quebec's northern boundary
    (1898), 36
Bourassa, Robert, 102
Bracken, John, 51
British, 23, 25, 26-27
British Columbia, 38, 74, 101
    and Confederation, 34

fur trade, 26
    and the Yukon, 42-43, 44
British Columbia Railway, 51

Calder Case, 109
Calgary, 115
Canadian National Railway, 50
Canadian Pacific Railway, 48, 50
Canadian Shield, 11, 12, 16
CANOL project, 63, 64
Carboniferous period, 11
Cariboo district, 47
Cariboo Road, 47
Cartier, Jacques, 24
Cassiar, 47, 97
Champlain, Samuel de, 24
Chicoutimi, 58
Chisasibi, 102, 106
Chruchill Forest Industries, 99
Church of England, 28
Churchill, 48, 50, 61, 64, 65
Churchill River (Labrador), 3, 15,
    101
Churchill River (Manitoba), 15, 40
Coal, 3, 16, 98
Cobalt, 49
Cochrane, 50, 71
Colonialism, 116-117, 130
Company of Adventurers Trading
    into Hudson Bay. See
    Hudson's Bay Company
Copper, 16, 48, 49, 52, 93
"Cultural materialism," 23
Cumberland House, 27, 69

Daishowa Canada, 100
Davis, Bill, 120-121
Dawson City, 87
Dawson Creek, 6, 56, 57, 63, 64,
    66, 91
Dease Lake, 47, 48, 69
Dease-Liard region, 90
Deibel, Ed, 120-121

Dempster Highway, 87
Denison Mine, 92, 96
Devine, Grant, 89
Diamond, Chief Billy, 102
Diefenbaker, John, 4, 86-88
Dinsdale, Walter, 88
Dobyns, Henry, 25
Dolbeau district, 55
Dryden, 58
Duncan, William, 29
Dutch, 25

Eastmain, 69
Eastmain River, 15, 36
Edmonton, 53, 56, 64
Educational achievement, 106.
    See also Native people, and
    mission schools
Elliot Lake, 62, 92-97, 111
Environment, conservation, 73-74
Environmental movement-Native
    coalition, 119, 121-122
Escoumains, 82
Estay Creek, 114

Fairbanks, Alaska, 64
Finlay River, 34
First Nations people. See Native
    people
Fishing, 76
Flin Flon, 50, 52, 90
Fly-in camps, 117, 130
Forest industry, 75, 98-100
Fort Chipewyan, 79
Fort Churchill, 16, 25
Fort Garry, 27
Fort George (B. C.), 28
Fort George (Quebec), 69, 102
Fort McMurray, 97, 114, 128
Fort Nelson, 51, 64, 69, 97
Fort Severn, 69
Fort St. John, 6, 16, 27, 53, 56, 64,
    66, 97
Fort Vermilion, 69
Fort William, 58, 120
Foster, Brigadier-General W. W.,
    65
Fraser, Simon, 27
Fraser Lake, 34
Fraser River valley, 34, 47
French, 25-26
Fur trade, 25-32
    American traders, 27

impact on Native people, 29-31
merger of Hudson's Bay
    Company and North West
    Company, 28
Montreal traders, 26, 27
Native people and European ri-
    valry, 26
Russian traders, 26

Garden River, 82
German-Canadian internees, 65
Gitskan territory, 119
Gold, 16, 34, 47-48, 49-50, 52, 92,
    98
Gold Mining Assistance Act, 98
Goose Bay, 65
Grande Prairie, 56-57
Grant, Shelagh, 65
Grassy Narrows, 105
Great Plains, 16
Great Slave Railway, 51
Great Whale River, 3, 15
Green, Sidney, 110
Greenpeace, 121, 122
Grey Nuns, 79
Gulf of St. Lawrence, 23

Haines Highway, 63
Hamelin, Louis-E., 6
Hamilton, Alvin, 88
Harper, Elijah, 4
Harris, Cole, 47
Harris, Marvin, 23
Hart Highway, 91
Hayes River, 15
Hazelton, 82
Hebron, 128
Hémon, Louis, 55
Hind, Henry Youle, 54
Hobbes, Thomas, 20
Hollinger mines, 49
Housing (conditions), 91
Howe, C. D., 3
Hudson Bay, 13, 40
Hudson Bay Mining and Smelt-
    ing, 52
Hudson Bay Railway, 50
Hudson Strait, 13, 40
Hudson Straits, 50
Hudson's Bay Company, 25, 26,
    27, 28, 30, 31, 32, 70-71, 72-73, 122
Hudson's Hope, 101
Hunting, 75, 76
Huronia, 120

Hydro-electric development, 100-103, 110
Hydro-electricity, 59
Hydro-Québec, 101

Indian Act, 78, 82
Indian Affairs, Department of, 82
Indians. *See* Native people
Indigenous people. *See* Native people
International Nickel Company, 50
Interprovincial Conference of Ministries Responsible for Northern Development, 128
Iron ore, 16, 48, 92
Iron Ore Company of Canada, 93
Island Falls, 52, 59
Italian-Canadian internees, 65

James Bay, 48
James Bay and Northern Quebec Agreement, 89
James Bay Project, 3, 102, 110
James Bay regions, 40
Japan, 96
Japanese capital, 100
Japanese industry, 98
Judicial Committee of the Privy Council, 35, 36, 37

Keewatin, 13
Keewatin district, 36
Kehoe, Alice, 18-19, 28-29
Kemano Dam, 115, 127
Kenora (Ontario), 99, 126
King, William Lyon Mackenzie, 4, 43
Kirkland Lake, 49, 62, 91, 92, 98
Kitimat, 93, 111
Klondike, 42, 53
Klondike gold rush, 47, 91

Labelle, Father F. X. A., 55
Labrador, 15, 23, 35, 53-54, 74
Labrador City, 92, 111
Lac La Ronge, 69
Lake Athabasca, 92, 101
Lake Timiskaming, 48
Lake Timiskaming district, 56
Lake of the Woods, 36
L'Anse aux Meadows, 23
Laurentide Air Northern Aerial Mining Exploring, 90
Laurier, Wilfrid, 37-38

Lesage, Jean, 101
Lévesque, René, 101
Limbrick, Hubert, 120
Lower Post, (B. C.), 47
Lynne Lake, 93

Macdonald, John A., 87
Mackenzie, Alexander, 27
Mackenzie River, 42, 53
Mackenzie River valley, 63
Mackenzie Valley, 12, 13
Manion, Robert, 3
Manitoba, 36-37, 40, 51
Manitoba Hydro, 110
Manitoba provincial boundaries, 36-37
Manitoulin, 56
Meech Lake Accord, 44
Mercury poisoning, 106
Methy Portage, 27
Middle North. *See* Provincial Norths
Migratory Birds Convention Treaty, 74
Minaki, 90
Missionaries, 78, 81-82
Mistassini River, 55
Montreal, 25, 115
Moose Factory, 16
Moose River, 102
Moosonee, 14, 50, 69
Moravians, 29, 79
Morton, W. L., 6
Mulroney, Brian, 93

Nain, 108, 128
Native people,
  Algonkian, 19, 22
  attitude towards resource development, 123-124
  Beaver, 23
  Beothuk, 23
  Carrier, 19
  Chief of the York Factory band, 83-84
  Chipewyan, 25
  Chipewyan Beaver, 19
    and Christianity, 81-82
    and confrontation over resource development, 102, 109, 111, 115, 118, 119
  Cree, 2, 19, 25, 26, 28-29
    and crime, 77-78
    cultures of, 22-23

Dene (Athapaskan), 19, 22
and discrimination, 75
Dorset and Thule peoples, 18
and economic dislocation,
107-108
entrepreneurship, 108-109
and the federal government, 83-
84
five basic groups, 19
and the fur economy, 70-73, 76,
77
Gitskan Wet'suwet'en, 3, 119
and government conservation
policies, 74-75
history of early contact period,
24-32
and impact of Confederation, 69-
70
impact of fur trade, 29-31
Inganeka, 3
Inland Tlingit, 19
Innu, 2, 19, 29, 115, 119
Inuit, 19, 20, 22, 23, 29, 79, 119
James Bay Cree, 102, 106, 108,
110, 119, 124
Lubicon, 3, 119, 124
Manitoba Cree, 102
and mission schools, 69, 78-81
Montagnais, 19, 24, 25, 29
Moose River Band, 102
Naskapi, 19, 23, 24, 25, 29
Nipissings, 79
Nisga'a, 19, 109
and "numbered" treaties, 83
Ojibwa, 19, 23, 25, 26, 28-29
population at time of European
contact, 21
pre-contact history, 18-23
and race relations, 76-78
residents of Grassy Narrows,
105
Southern Indian Lake residents,
110
Tahltan, 19
Teme-Augama Anishnabi, 3, 115
Tsimshian, 19, 22, 29
and wage labour, 75-76
and the welfare state, 105-107
women and male-dominated
leadership, 110
Woodlands Cree, 23
Natural gas, 97
Natural resources, control of, 51
Nelson River, 15

Nelson River Development, 110
New Brunswick, 34, 35
New France, 25, 27, 35
New Liskeard, 91, 92
"New Ontario," 120
Newfoundland, 35, 65, 89, 100,
101
Nicholson, Norman, 39
Nickel, 48, 50, 93
Northeast Coal Project, 98
Northern Affairs, Ontario Minis-
try of, 89
Northern Alberta Development
Corporation, 89
Northern Ontario Railway, 48, 50
Northern resource towns, 116-117
Northern Saskatchewan, 53-54
Northern Saskatchewan, Depart-
ment of, 89
Northern secession, 120-121
Noranda, 49, 62
Norman Wells, 53, 64
Norse, 23
North Bay, 120 North Shore (Que-
bec), 92
North West Company, 27, 28
North-West Territories, 34, 35
Northwest Defence Projects, 63
Northwest Staging Route, 63
Northwest Territories, 4, 44, 51
Norway House, 27, 69
Nouveau Québec, 13, 15, 16, 93,
125
Nova Scotia, 34, 35
Nunavut, 2, 44

Oil, 53. *See also* petroleum
Oleson, T., 23, 24
Ontario, 34, 89
northern expansion, 38-39, 40
Ontario Heritage Party, 120-121
Ontario Hydro, 96, 97
Osborne, Kitty, 126

Pacific Great Eastern Railway, 51,
91
Paine, Robert, 104
Palliser, John, 54
Patricia district, 61
Pattullo, T. "Duff," 42-43
Peace River, 101
Peace River country, 13, 15, 56
Peace River valley, 40

Peace River-Lake Athabasca region, 100
Petroleum, 97
Phelps, Joe, 88-89
Pickering, 96
Pine Point Mine, 91
Pollution, 48, 99-100, 106
Pond, Peter, 27
Port Arthur, 36, 58
Port Cartier, 92
Portuguese, 23
Precambrian age, 11
Prince Albert, 54
Prince Albert National Park, 74
Prince George, 51, 91, 99
Prince Rupert, 90
Project Crimson, 64
Project North, 113
Protestant churches, 184
Provincial Norths,
    climate, 16
    definition, 13-14, 17
    economic development of, 46-60, 90, 92
    flora and fauna, 16
    and impact of World War II, 63-67
    internal colonies, 6, 45, 60
    and internal political boundaries, 40-42
    and the lack of a common identity, 125-131
    and the lack of political influence, 60-62
    landforms, 13-15
    pattern of development, 46-47
    problem of definition, 1, 6-9
Pukaskwa National Park, 74
Pukatawagan, 107

Quebec, 34, 35, 40, 89, 101, 101-102
    northern expansion, 38-39, 40
Quebec (French settlement), 25

Racial tensions, 126
Rainbow region, 97
Ray, A. J., 30-31, 73
Red Lake, 90
Red River, 27, 28
Red River valley, 36
Regina, 108
Reid, Escott, 86
Retirement Living Program, 96

Rio Algom, 96
Robinson-Huron and Robinson-Superior Treaties, 32, 83
Rocky Mountains, 14
Rohmer, Richard, 4, 14
Roman Catholic church, 184
    and agricultural colonies, 54-55
Roman Catholic priests, 29
Rouyn, 90, 111
Rupert's Land, 28, 36
Rural Agricultural and Northern Development, Department of, 89

Saddle Lake, 82
Sahlins, Marshall, 20-21
Salmon canneries, 76
Santayana, George, 126
Saskatchewan, 40, 51, 89
    and northern expansion, 38
Saskatchewan district, 37
Sault Ste. Marie, 56
Scheffer, Lionel, 93
Schefferville, 91, 92-93, 93, 111
Secession. *See* Northern secession
Secrétariat des Activités gouvernementals en milieu Amerindien et Inuit, 89
Sept-Îles, 92
Seven Sisters, 59
Shamattawa, 128
Shawinigan Falls, 58
Shawinigan Water and Power, 59
Sherritt-Gordon Company, 53, 93
Sheshatshit, 128
Silver, 48, 49, 92
Simpson, George, 28
Sioux Lookout, 14, 90
Sisco mine, 49
Skeena River, 15
Ski-Doo, 90
Slave Falls, 59
Smallwood, Joey, 100, 100-101
Smithers, 111
Social disruptions, 106-107
Soldier Settlement Board, 56
Stickeen (Stikine) Territory, 34
Stikine country, 47
Stikine River, 15
St. Lawrence River, 40
St. Lawrence River valley, 13
Sub-Arctic. *See* Provincial Norths
Sudbury, 48, 91, 92, 120
Summer Beaver, 108
Swan Hills, 97

Swan River Valley, 54

Telegraph Creek, 47, 108
Temiscamingue, 56
Territorial North, 61, 63, 66
The Pas, 58, 64, 99, 111, 126
Thompson, 50, 62, 92, 111
Thorold, 58
Thunder Bay, 6-7, 16, 48, 58, 99
Timmins, 14, 49, 62, 92, 98, 111
Tolmie, Simon Fraser, 60
Toronto, 108, 115
Trapping, 75, 76
Tumbler Ridge, 62, 98, 111

Unemployment, 107
Ungava and Mackenzie, district
    of, 37
Ungava Peninsula, 14
United Church, 80, 119
Uranium, 16, 95-97
Uranium City, 92, 111

Val d'Or, 49
Vancouver, 108, 115

W. A. C. Bennett Dam, 3, 101
Wabush, 92
Welfare colonialism, 103-105
Western Canada, 37-38
White Paper, 104, 109
Whitehorse, 64
Winnipeg, 108, 115
Wisconsin (glaciation period), 12
Wood Buffalo National Park, 74
World War II, and impact on the
    North, 63-66

York Factory, 25, 69
Yukon, 4, 34, 44, 63

Zama region, 97
Zaslow, Morris, 48
Zinc, 52